30-DAY Drum Workout

An Exercise Plan for Drummers

Pete Sweeney

National Guitar Workshop Book

Approved Curriculum

Alfred, the leader in educational publishing, and the National Guitar Workshop, one of Amercia's finest guitar schools, have joined forces to bring you the best, most progressive educational tools possible. We hope you will enjoy this book and encourage you to look for other fine products from Alfred and the National Guitar Workshop.

This book was acquired, edited and produced by Workshop Arts, Inc., the publishing arm of the National Guitar Workshop.
Nathaniel Gunod, editor
Gary Tomassetti, music typesetter
Timothy Phelps, interior design

Alfred Publishing Co., Inc.
16320 Roscoe Blvd., Suite 100
P.O. Box 10003
Van Nuys, CA 91410-0003
alfred.com

ISBN-10: 0-7390-1074-3 (Book)
ISBN-13: 978-0-7390-1074-7 (Book)

ISBN-10: 0-7390-3826-5 (DVD)
ISBN-13: 978-0-7390-3826-0 (DVD)

ISBN-10: 0-7390-3827-3 (Book and DVD)
ISBN-13: 978-0-7390-3827-7 (Book and DVD)

Contents

About the Author

Pete Sweeney has been a professional musician since 1983. He studied with Dave Calarco, Joe Morello and other notable drummers. He also attended the Drummer's Collective of New York City.

Pete has been a faculty member at the National Guitar Workshop since 1993. He has performed with Duke Robillard, Ronnie Earl, Mick Goodrick, Frank Gambale, Nick Brignola, Vinnie Moore and many others.

Additionally, he has toured the United States with various musical groups and has appeared on numerous CDs featuring a variety of musical styles from the "Big Band" era to rock'n'roll, funk, blues and jazz.

Pete performed on a Grammy-nominated CD with the Jay Traynor Big Band, and on the soundtrack for the Miramax film, "The Castle." He has toured nationally with Tony Kenny of Ireland, and with "Dangerous" Dan Toler.

Pete Sweeney endorses Vic Firth sticks, Aquarian drum heads and Sabian cymbals.

Pete lives in Chatham, New York.

Acknowledgements

I would like to thank: Neil Larrivee, Terry Shaw and Bob Boos of Sabian; my teachers, Dave Calarco and Joe Morello; Chris Brady and Roy Burns of Aquarian; Neil Larrivee of Vic Firth; my parents, Patrick and Patricia Sweeney; my brother Paul; my wife, Robin; and Nat Gunod and Dave Smolover of the National Guitar Workshop.

Introduction

Welcome to the *30-Day Drum Workout*. This book is designed to help you in many ways. It will provide a solid practice routine that covers various aspects of drum-set technique. These techniques will help you with speed, endurance, accuracy, consistency and fluidity. Because of the nature of the instrument, we drummers are playing almost constantly in any given performance. Therefore, practicing technique is a way to insure that we are going to be in shape for the gig and uphold our obligation to the time. This is no easy matter! It requires a consistent commitment to practicing that addresses long-term goals. This book will help by providing a clear, easy-to-follow routine of interesting and essential exercises for the hands (Hand Fitness exercises) and the feet (Set Fitness exercises). These exercises can— and should—be used for all styles of music. Whether you play heavy metal or jazz, all of these techniques can be adapted to your particular situation.

There are two workouts in this book. The Proficiency Workout is for intermediate-level players, and The Extended Proficiency Workout is for more advanced drummers. Advanced drummers should take a good look at The Proficiency Workout too—you may find that it will help fill some gaps in your training. If you are using The Proficiency Workout and it ceases to challenge you, move on to The Extended Proficiency Workout.

There are several ways you can use this book:
1. Learn the warm-ups and go right through the 30-Day course as prescribed.
2. Look for exercises that remedy specific problems you may be having.
3. Work on just the hand exercises.
4. Work on just the foot exercises.
5. Work on just the full set exercises.
6. Just use the warm-up exercises.
7. Play all exercises using the brushes.

Start by spending about a week on the warm-up exercises. This will provide you with a good foundation for the workouts that will follow. Next, begin learning the individual workouts. Where there is more than one exercise on a particular day, take your time and be sure you have control over the primary exercise before you move on to the others, which build on the original concept. This may take more than one day, so don't be in a hurry to get to the end! You will find that this material is more beneficial after you have spent some time fine-tuning it. Be patient and it will happen.

After you have been through the workouts once, you will know how to customize your workout. That may mean looking for consistent weaknesses in your own playing and finding exercises to remedy them. You should also spend time creating variations of your own based on the principals put forth in this book. This will make practicing more enjoyable and help your own creativity. As with any material, you are basically *learning how to learn*. Hopefully, the system presented here will help in organizing your practice time so that there isn't time wasted in the practice room.

> ### *DO NOT SPEND ALL YOUR TIME ON THIS MATERIAL!*
> Technique is only a means to an end. The end result is playing music, so don't spend all of your time on technique. This material will help you learn *how* to play, not *what* to play. You will play what you *hear* and what you *practice*, so strive to achieve a balance in the material you work on.

Section One Reading and Terminology

Before we begin with the workouts, let's spend a few moments looking at the fundamentals of rhythmic notation for the drums. This will help in learning the exercises that follow and can be used as a reference later.

Note Values

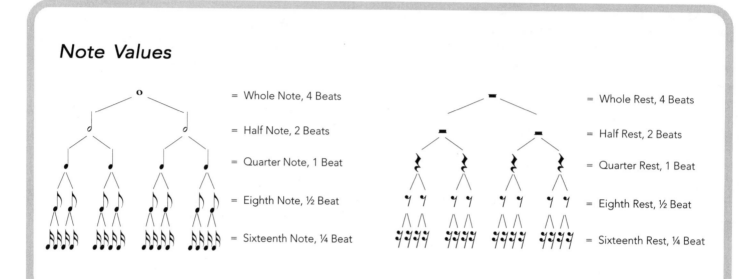

= Whole Note, 4 Beats

= Half Note, 2 Beats

= Quarter Note, 1 Beat

= Eighth Note, ½ Beat

= Sixteenth Note, ¼ Beat

= Whole Rest, 4 Beats

= Half Rest, 2 Beats

= Quarter Rest, 1 Beat

= Eighth Rest, ½ Beat

= Sixteenth Rest, ¼ Beat

The Staff and Measures

All the music in this book is written on a group of five lines called a *staff*. Using *bar lines*, the staff is divided into *measures*. Each measure will contain a certain number of beats. The *clef* sign tells you it's drum music, although you may see the bass clef 𝄢 sign used in some publications. A *double bar* is sometimes used to show the end of an example or section.

Clef   Bar Lines   Double bar

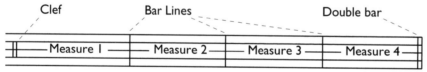

—Measure 1 —   — Measure 2 —   — Measure 3 —   — Measure 4 —

At the beginning of each exercise, you will see a *time signature*. The top number tells you how many beats are in each measure; the bottom number tells you what kind of note gets one beat.

4 Four beats per measure
4 The quarter note ♩ gets one beat

There will be examples in this book that are not in ⁴⁄₄ time, so be aware of the time signature. Here are some examples showing other time signatures:

Basic Drum Notation

Below is a key to understanding the drum set notation in this book. The system is very logical in that it reflects the way your drums are set up: the cymbals are on top, the first tom and second tom are on the next space and line down, the snare is in the middle and the floor tom and bass drum are on the bottom.

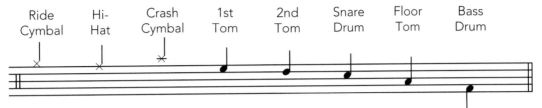

Repeat Signs

The *repeat sign* means to repeat the measure or measures again. Play these two measures twice.

There are a few effects that also need to be written. They include the open and closed hi-hat and the hi-hat stepped with the foot.

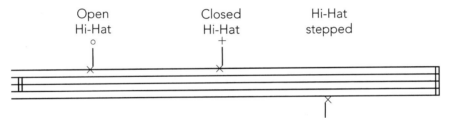

The Metronome

A metronome is an adjustable device used by musicians to keep steady time and to find specific tempos. It is very useful for checking the evenness of your note values and pinpointing problem areas as you practice. You should use a metronome as part of your daily practice routine. The exercises in this book will have suggested *tempos* (speeds). Begin studying each exercise at the indicated tempo (or slower). Then, as your confidence builds, work on getting faster. The tempos are only suggestions, and therefore are not set in stone. *It is always better to have consistent control at a slower tempo than to play fast without being in control.* The metronome will also help you measure your development from day to day, and can help you make steady improvements over time.

Metronomes measure tempos in beats per minute. So a tempo marking such as ♩ = 60 tells us to set the metronome speed to 60—sixty beats per minute.

Dynamics

SYMBOL	NAME	DEFINITION
pp	*pianissimo*	very soft
p	*piano*	soft
mf	*mezzo forte*	moderately loud
f	*forte*	loud
ff	*fortissimo*	very loud
⊏⊐	*crescendo*	gradually getting louder
⊐⊏	*decrecendo*	gradually getting softer

Section Two Basic Technique

In this section, we will take a look at basic hand and foot technique. We will also cover the basic strokes for accented and unaccented notes. This is the foundation for all of the workouts to follow.

Holding the Drumsticks

In theory, it should be easy to hold the drum sticks, but many times we make it more difficult than it needs to be. Always keep in mind that you want a natural approach to holding the sticks—they should be extensions of your hands. In the paragraphs that follow, we will investigate the two basic ways of holding the sticks.

The Matched Grip

In a *matched grip*, the right and left hands hold the sticks in exactly the same way. The thumb and index finger should grip the stick at the balance point (approximately five inches from the butt end). The stick will be balanced at the first knuckle of the index finger and the flat part of the thumb. Keep in mind that the stick should be gripped just enough to hold it securely but not squeezed or pinched. Squeezing too hard is an undesirable technique that can cause all kinds of hand problems, especially at high-volume situations where the drummer is really "hitting it." Be sure to keep the space between the thumb and index finger open, and the muscles relaxed.

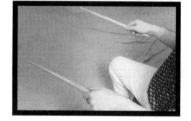

The Traditional Grip

In the *traditional grip*, the left hand holds the stick differently than the right hand. The right hand holds the stick as it did in the matched grip.

Place the left stick in the socket between the left thumb and first finger, with one third of top of the stick (from the butt end) extending behind the hand.

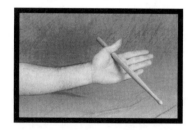

The first two fingers should rest lightly on the stick to act as a guide. The stick should rest across the 3rd finger as a support. The 4th finger should rest against the 3rd finger.

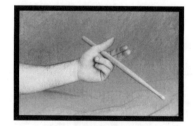

Bass Drum Technique

There are basically two techniques for playing the bass drum: *heel up* or *heel down* (flat-footed). Both are effective and both should be practiced equally. The heel-down technique is good for control in softer passages and feels good because, with the foot down on the pedal, the rest of the body feels balanced. It is also great for slower tempos for this reason. The heel-up method is great for playing at louder volumes because you have more power when using your whole leg to play the bass drum. It is also effective when you want to play fast, multiple notes. Because the leg is raised, the ankle has a chance to manipulate the foot in a looser fashion and achieve quicker bass drum beats.

Heel Up

Heel Down

Foot-Board Slide

This is a type of heel-up stroke that is used for playing rapid double strokes. We can get quick multiple notes by making an initial stroke with a downward motion and then sliding the foot forward on the second note. There will be exercises to follow that use this technique.

First Stroke   Slide to Second Stroke

Hi-Hat Technique

There are a number of ways to play the hi-hat. They are the *heel down* (flat foot), *heel up* and *side-to-side* techniques. As with the bass drum, all are valuable and should be practiced individually.

Heel Down   Heel Up

Side-to-Side

For the side-to-side technique, with the toe as your anchor, swing the heel back and forth (right to left) on each side of the pedal. This provides greater freedom of movement than the usual up and down motion, and will provide for greater endurance during long hi-hat passages.

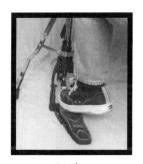 

Right   Left

Basic Strokes in Drumming

There are four frequently used strokes used in drumming. They are:

Full stroke
Down stroke
Tap stroke
Tap/up stroke

When we play, we use all of these motions constantly but usually on an unconscious level. Many drummers never break down these strokes in practice, so they often play in very unnatural ways. Generally, we are only aware of these strokes when something isn't working. If you have never studied this kind of material before, you should spend a few weeks working on it in a very focused manner. This kind of practice will pay off in a big way.

The Full Stroke

The *full stroke* is most often used for *accents* (a note played louder than the others around it). It begins with the tip of the stick pointed at the ceiling, or at a 90-degree angle. Throw the stick down to the drum and allow the stick to rebound back to its original position. You may feel the urge to physically bring the stick back to its original position. This is not necessary. The stick will return naturally, on its own, if you simply accept the rebound and control it. There is no pulling involved. It is much like dribbling a basketball—we throw the ball down and it rebounds on its own. Remember, for every action there is an equal and opposite reaction. If you throw the stick down at a certain velocity, it will respond by rebounding at an appropriate speed. The trick is to control that rebound and *use it* so we're not working hard to get results.

Down stroke

A *down stroke* is used to play an accented note when the next stroke is not accented. We start from a full stroke position, then strike the drum and keep the stick down low rather than let it rebound completely. When you strike, don't tense up your fingers or hand in an attempt to stop the stick. This is where many drummers hurt their hands—by freezing the stick as they make a stroke. It doesn't require that much tension to keep the stick from bouncing up. Notice how much tension and release is involved when practicing these strokes.

The Tap Stroke

The *tap stroke* is used for an unaccented note. We simply strike the drum from a lower level and allow the stick to rebound back to its original position. This is done primarily when the following note is also unaccented.

The Tap/Up Stroke

The *tap/up stroke* is used when playing an unaccented note followed by an accented note. Begin by playing the tap stroke and then raising the stick to a full stroke position after the tap has been made. This naturally prepares the hand for an accented note to follow.

Exercises Using the Different Strokes

Following are a few exercises using all of the strokes discussed in this section. Practice these slowly ($\quarternote$ = 60) and observe the stick height and other motions very closely. These strokes will help you make the difference between accented and unaccented notes more distinct and make them more natural to play.

#1

#2

F = Full stroke
D = Down stroke
T = Tap stroke
T/U = Tap/up stroke
> = accent

#3

Section Three Warm-Up Exercises

Hand Warm-Ups

Before you practice or perform, it is always a good idea to warm-up with exercises that loosen-up your chops. This section will provide a few to get you started. The idea is to warm-up gradually rather than jump right into a vigorous workout, so take the exercises slow and steady, then work up to faster tempos. Runners don't warm-up by starting out at their fastest speed—they stretch out for a while and eventually work up to speed. In this way, they avoid possible injury. Using the suggested tempos as a guide, we can apply the same principle to playing the drums.

Hand Warm-Up #1
The Single-Stroke Roll

Start by playing a single-stroke roll (one stroke per stick) with full strokes. Make sure that all the strokes are even in sound. Be sure to end every stroke at the same height from which you began. Do this at ♩ = 70 and continue for at least three minutes. Then, increase the tempo. This exercise will help loosen your wrists, forearms and biceps, and will reinforce an important concept for playing full strokes: always *play off the drum* rather than *into the drum*. In other words, let the stick rebound freely.

Now reverse the sticking so the roll starts with the left hand. If you are left-handed, you can choose to reverse all sticking instructions.

Hand Warm-Up #2
Double-Stroke Roll

Now let's play the double-stroke roll (two strokes per stick) with full strokes. Be sure that each stroke is the same height and sounds even. Start slowly (♩ = 70) and continue for three minutes. Gradually increase the tempo as your control over the double strokes improves.

Reverse the sticking and start with a left-hand lead.

Hand Warm-Up #3
Combining Double and Single Strokes

Play 4 times   Play 4 times

Now let's put the two types of strokes together in a combination exercise. Start with single strokes for four bars, followed by double strokes for four bars. Both the singles and the doubles should sound the same, with no change in *dynamics* (degree of loudness or softness). The secret is in keeping the height of the strokes even.

Hand Warm-Up #4
Continuous Eighth-Note Exercise

This exercise consists of playing continuous eighth notes with one hand for several minutes. This is a tremendous warm-up that is great for building endurance. Start with eighth notes in the right hand at a tempo of ♩ = 100. Play the eighths with full strokes from about 10 inches off the drum head or practice pad. Keep an eye on the direction of your strokes; you want them to be as straight as possible—directly down and up, with no sideways motion. Remember that the shortest distance between two points is a straight line. Do this for at least one minute, but stop and rest if you feel tension building in your arm or hand. Now play continuous eighths with the left hand. Again, practice this for a minimum of one minute. When you have completed this with both hands, move the tempo up by eight to ten beats per minute and repeat the exercise. Eventually, you will find a tempo at which your weaker hand cannot keep the eighth notes going for a full minute. When you arrive at this tempo, modify the exercise by playing eighths for only 30 seconds.

Since the point of this exercise is to build stamina, you should practice it for long periods of time. After doing this exercise for a few weeks, you will notice a big difference, especially with the weaker hand. Make sure you are paying attention to your wrist muscles; keep them relaxed and flexible. Feel free to extend the exercise longer as your endurance progresses.

Hand Warm-Up #5
Single-Stroke Roll

After completing Warm-Up #4, you may want to tag on an additional minute of a single-stroke roll in sixteenth notes. Whichever hand you worked with last in the continuous eighths becomes the lead hand for the single-stroke roll. Keep in mind that this should be done at tempos where both hands are capable of playing the exercise precisely. If one hand is having trouble, slow the tempo down to a point where both can hold the tempo with eighth notes in a relaxed way. Then add on an additional minute with single-stroke sixteenths.

Hand Warm-Up #6
Eighth- and Sixteenth-Note Singles

Another great warm-up is to play one bar of eighth notes and then one bar of sixteenth notes, all in single strokes. Then play another bar of eighth notes followed by *two* bars of sixteenth notes, still all in single strokes. Build this up until you are playing at least eight bars of sixteenth notes in single strokes to every one bar of eighth notes. You can play more if you wish, but eight bars is a good starting goal. As always, check for evenness. Start at ♩ = 88 and take the tempo up from there!

Continue

Set Warm-Ups

Here are a few exercises that will increase your stamina, flexibility and accuracy when playing the bass drum:

Set Warm-Up #1
Bass-Drum Pedaling in Eighths, Triplets and Sixteenths

Start by playing two bars of eighth notes followed by two bars of eighth-note *triplets* (three strokes per beat) and then two bars of sixteenth notes. Repeat this a minimum of eight times. A good beginning tempo is ♩ = 60. Try doing this and making sure the transitions from eighths to triplets and triplets to sixteenths are secure. Initially, do this exercise using heel-down bass pedal technique, letting the bass-drum beater come back six to seven inches from the bass drum head.

As you increase the tempo, it will feel better to raise your leg and play this with the heel-up technique. You will also need to decrease the distance of your stroke with the bass-drum pedal. Feel free to extend the number of measures or repetitions for each note value.

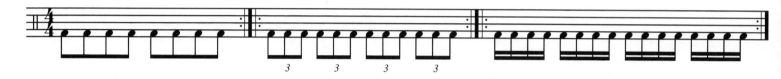

You may want to add a stepped hi-hat on quarter notes as you play this warm-up. You can move the stepped hi-hat from quarter notes to eighth notes as you work through the warm-up. This is great for coordination between the feet.

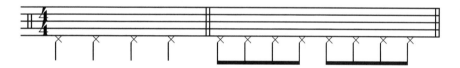

Set Warm-Up #2
Bass-Drum Accents

Here is an exercise for working on accents with the bass drum while playing continuous eighth notes. Start at ♩ = 80.

Now play accent variations. Make sure the accented and unaccented notes sound different. The trick is to play the unaccented notes much quieter, from close to the head, and to hit the accented notes hard, from further away. This is a tremendous warm-up for the foot. When your foot feels like it's going to fall off, stop!

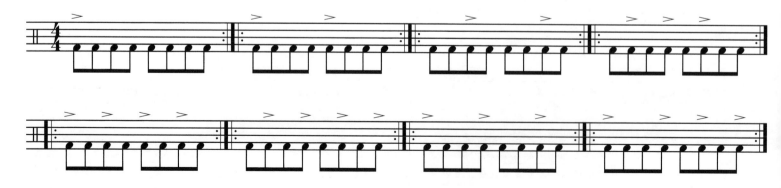

After we have warmed up with the hands and feet, it's time to move on to some exercises that use the whole drum set. Here is a series of exercises to increase fluidity when moving around the set:

Set Warm-Up #3
Clockwise Around the Set

This exercise has four sixteenth notes on each drum. Start this at ♩ = 88 and then gradually increase the tempo. Make sure your strokes are hitting the center of each drum.

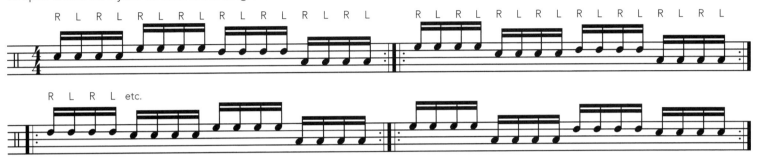

Set Warm-Up #4
Counter-Clockwise Around the Set

This exercise reverses the direction of Warm-Up #3. Watch for accuracy.

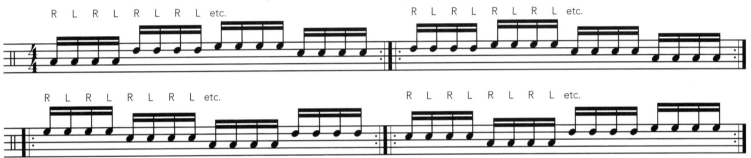

Set Warm-Up #5
Two Sixteenths per Drum

This exercise has *two* sixteenth notes on each drum.

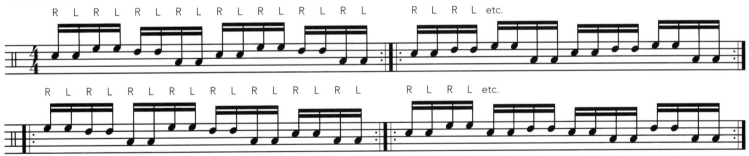

Set Warm-Up #6
Combinations

These are combinations of Warm-Ups #3, #4 and #5. Spend lots of time with these!

Section Four The Proficiency Workout

The workouts are divided into two categories, Hand Fitness and Set Fitness. Many of these workouts begin with a basic concept that is expanded upon in the next few days. Spend extra time with the original idea before moving on to the variations that follow. It may take a few days of practicing for some of these exercises to feel comfortable and under control. That's okay. There's no need to rush. Take the extra time and resolve any difficulties you may have. Here are a few suggestions for practicing these workouts:

1. Use a metronome and observe all of the suggested tempo markings. Start each exercise at the indicated tempo and then increase the speed from there. It is also a good idea to turn the metronome off, continue to play and then turn it back on to see if you stayed with the tempo. Do this often! Don't always rely on a constant click to develop your sense of time.

2. Keep a record of your practice activity. This is great for staying focused in the practice room. You can record your progress in a notebook and look back to see where and when you have improved.

3. Record yourself practicing. This enables you to listen back and immediately make adjustments to your performance. Record yourself playing with a metronome and listen to hear if you're playing with it accurately.

4. Use the warm-ups in the previous chapter before doing these workouts. You will feel much better having warmed up before any vigorous practice.

DAY ONE

Hand Warm-Ups #1-#6
Hand Fitness #1

This workout will improve your ability to accent any part of the beat of a single-stroke roll. These exercises are written with the different stroke motions for accented and unaccented notes. Start at ♩ = 70, then gradually increase the tempo.

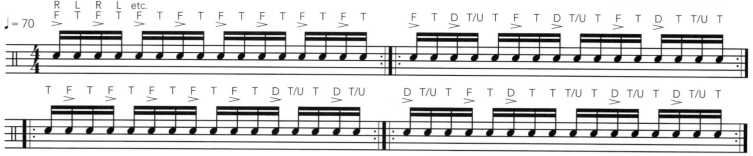

Set Warm-Ups #1-#6
Set Fitness #1

Take the accent patterns from Hand Fitness #1 and *double* (also play) all the accented notes on the bass drum. Make sure the snare and bass drum accents are played exactly together. Play quarter notes on the hi-hat.

30 DAY DRUM WORKOUT

1	2	3	4	5	6	7
8	9	10	11	12	13	14
15	16	17	18	19	20	21
22	23	24	25	26	27	28
29	30					

30 DAY DRUM WORKOUT						
1	2	3	4	5	6	7
8	9	10	11	12	13	14
15	16	17	18	19	20	21
22	23	24	25	26	27	28
29	30					

DAY TWO

Hand Warm-Ups #1–#6
Hand Fitness #2

Here are some more accents for the single-stroke roll. Stay relaxed and don't squeeze or pinch the sticks as you are making the accents. Much of the volume will come from the height of the sticks as you are making the strokes.

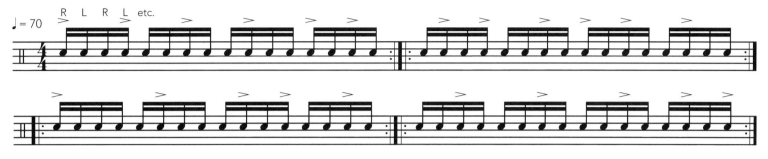

These accent patterns have two accented sixteenth notes in succession. Make sure the accents are clear and focused, with lots of contrast between loud and soft, before you push the tempo up.

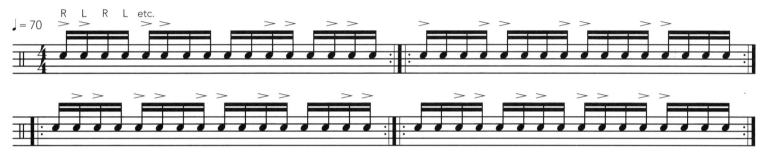

Set Warm-Ups #1–#6
Set Fitness #2

Let's take the accent ideas you've been working on and apply them to the drum set in two ways. The first will be to play all accents on the toms. Play the right-handed accents on the floor tom and the left-handed accents on the small tom. All unaccented strokes will be played on the snare drum. Play quarter notes on the bass drum, adding the hi-hat on beats 2 and 4.

The second way we can use these accent patterns is to place all accents on the crash cymbals doubled with the bass drum. Once again, the unaccented strokes are played on the snare drum.

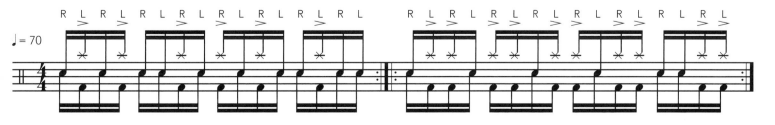

DAY THREE

Hand Warm-Ups #1-#6
Hand Fitness #3

This workout starts with four different stickings for the double-stroke roll. Listen for the evenness of your doubles, especially the second stroke. Don't rely on merely bouncing the second stroke, but make it a wrist stroke with the same height and volume as the first.

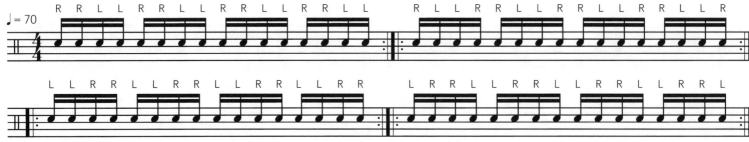

Let's take the first sticking and add accents. This will help you develop the evenness of your strokes, and will improve your ability to accent anywhere in the double-stroke roll.

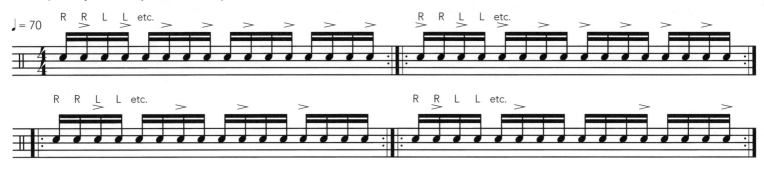

Set Warm-Ups #1-#6
Set Fitness #3

A great way to use doubles is to break them up around the set. Here is the first sticking of the double-stroke roll (RRLL) broken up between different drums.

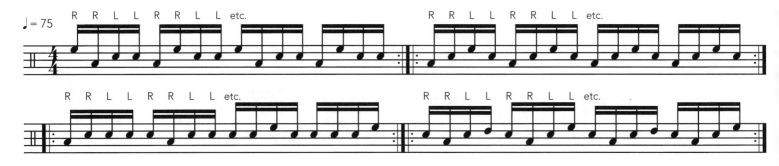

Here is a workout that uses broken-up doubles with a changing sticking pattern. This will get you moving around the set in some very interesting ways.

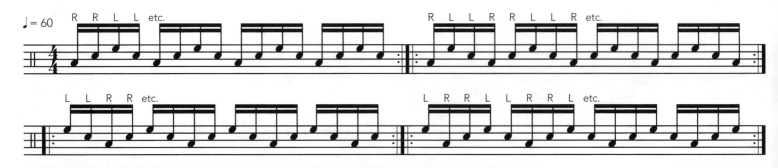

DAY FOUR

30 DAY DRUM WORKOUT						
1✓	2✓	3✓	4✓	5	6	7
8	9	10	11	12	13	14
15	16	17	18	19	20	21
22	23	24	25	26	27	28
29	30					

Hand Warm-Ups #1-#6
Hand Fitness #4

This warm-up has some accent patterns that will help your double-stroke roll. They all include two successive accented notes. This will get your doubles in shape and allow you to hear different possibilities for varying the roll. Start at ♩ = 70 and gradually increase the tempo.

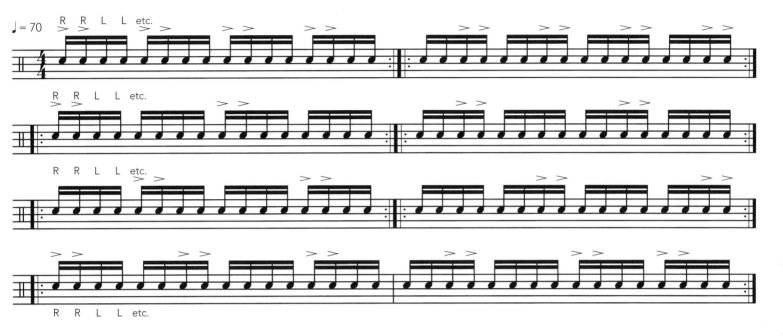

Set Warm-Ups #1-#6
Set Fitness #4

This warm-up puts some of the double accents on the drum set. Play quarter notes on the bass drum and add the hi-hat on beats 2 and 4. Strive for clear contrast between accented and non-accented notes.

(bass and hi-hat continue)

DAY FIVE

Hand Warm-Ups #1-#6
Hand Fitness #5

30 DAY DRUM WORKOUT

1	2	3	4	5	6	7
8	9	10	11	12	13	14
15	16	17	18	19	20	21
22	23	24	25	26	27	28
29	30					

Here is an exercise to get your *flams* in shape. A flam is played by slipping a quick stroke in just before the main stroke. For example, to flam a right-hand stroke, play a quick left-hand stroke directly before it. These quick notes are written as small *grace* notes. For this warm-up, play a flam roll with a left/right sticking for at least one minute before moving up the tempo. Remember to keep the grace-note stick as close to the drum as possible to get a good flam sound. Start slowly and gradually get the tempo up as fast as you can.

Set Warm-Ups #1-#6
Set Fitness #5

Go back to the double accent exercise (Hand Fitness #4 on page 19) and double the accented notes with the bass drum. The first two examples are written out here. Play quarter notes on the hi-hat.

DAY SIX

Hand Warm-Ups #1-#6
Hand Fitness #6

30 DAY DRUM WORKOUT

1	2	3	4	5	6	7
8	9	10	11	12	13	14
15	16	17	18	19	20	21
22	23	24	25	26	27	28
29	30					

This workout starts with a single-stroke roll for four bars, followed by a double-stroke roll for four bars and finally the flam roll for four bars. Start this at the indicated tempo and continue for at least one minute before trying to go faster.

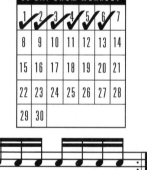

Set Warm-Ups #1-#6
Set Fitness #6

Here is an exercise to get that bass drum foot moving! Play a continuous single-stroke roll on the snare drum as you play these variations on the bass drum. Play each example twice and move on to the next without stopping. (Stop if your leg begins to cramp.) Try using both heel-up and heel-down bass-drum techniques. This becomes a real challenge when you play at a rapid tempo.

30 DAY DRUM WORKOUT						
1✓	2✓	3✓	4✓	5✓	6✓	7✓
8	9	10	11	12	13	14
15	16	17	18	19	20	21
22	23	24	25	26	27	28
29	30					

DAY SEVEN

Hand Warm-Ups #1-#6
Hand Fitness #7

This workout will give you better facility with the *paradiddle*. A paradiddle is nothing more than a combination of single and double strokes. This first exercise has four different paradiddle stickings. Start at the indicated tempo and increase it gradually. Listen for evenness of the hands and make the transitions from one sticking to another smooth and relaxed.

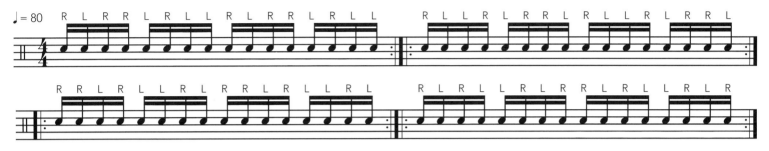

Now let's take the first sticking (RLRR LRLL) and add accents. As always, observe the motion and height of your strokes and work for good contrast between accented and unaccented notes.

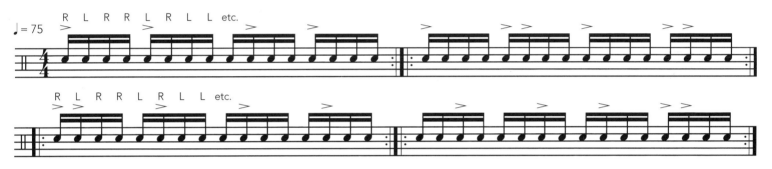

Here's a two-bar phrase that uses the paradiddle sticking:

Set Warm-Ups #1-#6
Set Fitness #7

Let's take the accents you worked on for the paradiddle and use them around the set. All accents will be played with the crash cymbals and the bass drum. Right-hand accents are played on the right crash, left-hand accents on the left crash and all unaccented notes are on the snare. Play quarter notes on the hi-hat throughout.

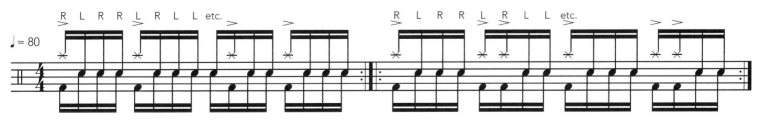

30 DAY DRUM WORKOUT						
1 ✓	2 ✓	3 ✓	4 ✓	5 ✓	6 ✓	7 ✓
8 ✓	9	10	11	12	13	14
15	16	17	18	19	20	21
22	23	24	25	26	27	28
29	30					

DAY EIGHT

Hand Warm-Ups #1-#6
Hand Fitness #8

In this workout, we will focus on accenting triplets with single-stroke-roll sticking. This will help you develop the ability to place an accent anywhere in the triplet, especially the ever difficult second note. Start this workout at the indicated tempo and work it up to a Buddy Rich tempo (*very fast*)!

Set Warm-Ups #1-#6
Set Fitness #8

This exercise uses those triplet accents on the set. One way is to double all the accents with the bass drum. The first two bars are written out, and you can continue the exercise by referring to Hand Fitness #8 above. The difficulty will be the simultaneous accents in the bass drum and the hand on the second note of the triplet. Counting aloud will help you stay in time.

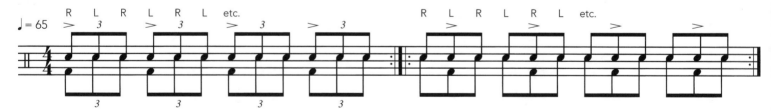

Another way to use these accents is to put them on the toms. All right-handed accents are on the floor tom, all left-handed accents are on the small tom. Play quarter notes with the bass drum and add the hi-hat on beats 2 and 4. The last two bars are written out here, but you can refer to Hand Fitness #8 above to do the whole exercise.

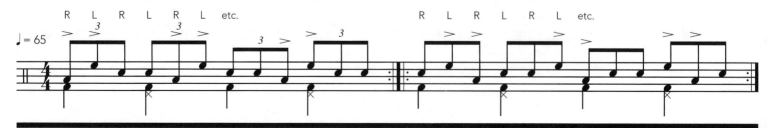

DAY NINE

30 DAY DRUM WORKOUT						
1 ✓	2 ✓	3 ✓	4 ✓	5 ✓	6 ✓	7 ✓
8 ✓	9 ✓	10	11	12	13	14
15	16	17	18	19	20	21
22	23	24	25	26	27	28
29	30					

Hand Warm-Ups #1-#6
Hand Fitness #9

This is a continuation of Hand Fitness #8. The idea is to embellish the accent by using a flam, a double stroke or a *buzz* (a multiple-stroke roll—more than two bounces on a stroke, not controlled as in a double stroke). First, let's play all of the accents using a flam. Here's what the first two bars look like with flams:

Now play the accented notes in Hand Fitness #8 as sixteenth-note double strokes. Accent both notes of each double. Here are the third and fourth bars written out:

$\not\equiv$ = Buzz Roll

Play all the accents as buzzes. The fifth and sixth bars are written out.

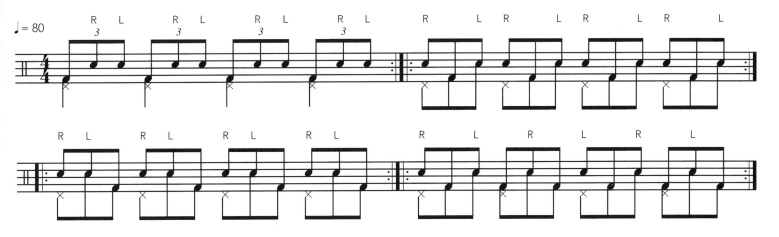

Set Warm-Ups #1-#6
Set Fitness #9

This exercise has some hand and foot combinations in triplets. The idea is to play these with a good flow between the snare and bass drum. Don't accent the snare stroke. Play quarter notes on the hi-hat.

DAY TEN

Hand Warm-Ups #1-#6
Hand Fitness #10

Today's workout will help you achieve better control with the six-stroke roll. We'll begin by focusing on two stickings for triplets: RLL and RRL. If you are left-handed, just reverse all the instructions.

Below are four stickings for the six-stroke roll. Begin these exercises by playing each one a few times without accents to master the transitions. Then add the accents and emphasize them strongly. Notice that the stickings and the shifting of the pairs of accented notes will enable you to hear and control the six-stroke roll with several different beginnings and endings. This will give you more options in performance.

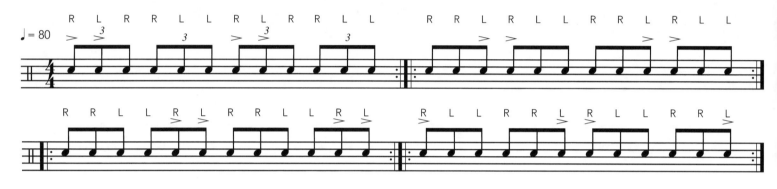

Set Warm-Ups #1-#6
Set Fitness #10

This exercise applies the six-stroke roll to the set by replacing the pairs of accented strokes with the bass drum. As you are practicing this, be sure that the bass drum notes sound evenly. When you play this faster, try using the heel-up and footboard-slide techniques with the bass drum (see page 9).

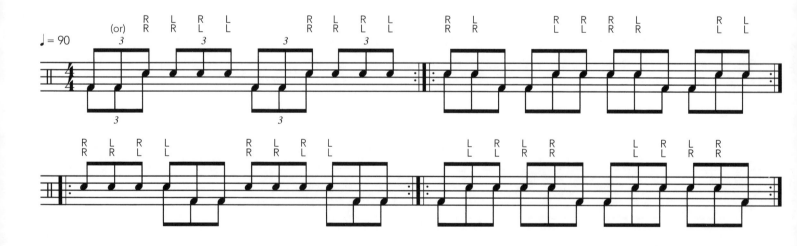

DAY ELEVEN

Hand Warm-Ups #1-#6
Hand Fitness #11

30 DAY DRUM WORKOUT						
1✓	2✓	3✓	4	5✓	6✓	7✓
8✓	9✓	10✓	11	12	13	14
15	16	17	18	19	20	21
22	23	24	25	26	27	28
29	30					

A great way to improve your six-stroke roll is to play a few bars of the roll as eighth-note triplets and a few bars as sixteenth-note triplets (three sixteenths per eighth note, or six notes per beat). Think of it as double-timing the figure using the exact same stickings and accents. Let's use the first six-stroke roll exercise from Hand Fitness #10 (page 24). As you get more control over the sixteenth-note triplets, go ahead and increase the number of bars you play using them.

Set Warm-Ups #1-#6
Set Fitness #11

Let's take Set Fitness #10 and embellish the phrase by adding double-stroke sixteenth-note triplets to the snare drum part. The first part of the exercise is shown below. Try playing the figure as it is written in Set Fitness #10 for two bars and then play it with the double-stroke sixteenth-note triplets for two bars.

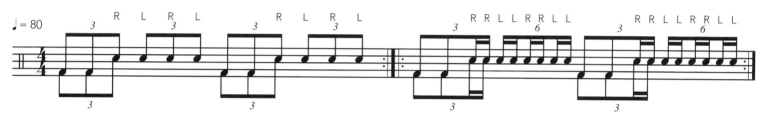

DAY TWELVE

Hand Warm-Ups #1-#6
Hand Fitness #12

Set Warm-Ups #1-#6
Set Fitness #12

30 DAY DRUM WORKOUT						
1✓	2✓	3✓	4✓	5✓	6✓	7✓
8✓	9✓	10✓	11✓	12	13	14
15	16	17	18	19	20	21
22	23	24	25	26	27	28
29	30					

Today is a review day. Take time today to review all of the material you have worked on so far. Work on the exercises with different dynamics and try increasing the tempos. The workouts that follow will be getting more difficult, so take the extra time to work on the basic techniques. Always keep a notebook handy so that you can write down any ideas or variations that you come up with as you practice.

DAY THIRTEEN

Hand Warm-Ups #1-#6
Hand Fitness #13

Here's a workout that's going to get your left hand in shape! The idea is to emphasize the weaker hand by progressively adding more strokes for it to play every four bars. Try starting this workout at a medium-slow tempo and concentrate on the motion of the left wrist. When you get this going faster, try playing the first stroke of the left hand as a wrist motion and the following strokes with the fingers. Don't tighten up in an attempt to play longer or faster. You want the left hand to be loose and flexible, with a minimum of tension. Start at the indicated tempo and increase your speed and stamina.

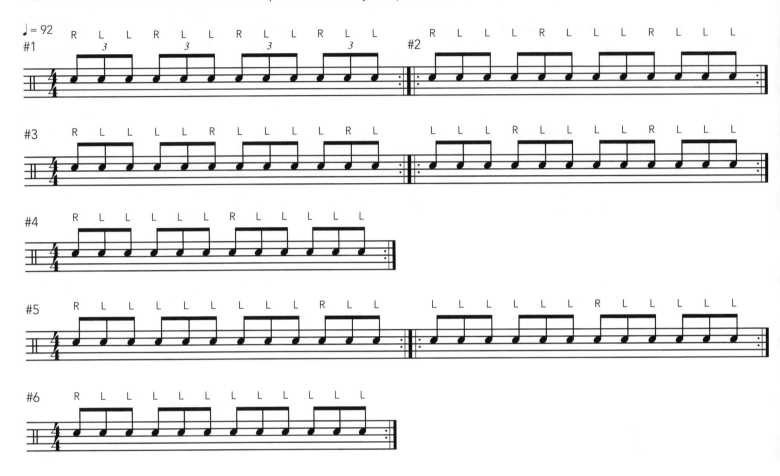

Set Warm-Ups #1-#6
Set Fitness #13

Here are some exercises to work on for getting around the full set. Sixteenth-note triplets are grouped with two single strokes on each drum. Play quarter notes on the bass drum, adding the hit-hat on beats 2 and 4. Use single-stroke roll sticking.

DAY FOURTEEN

Hand Warm-Ups #1-#6
Hand Fitness #14

Today's workout will give you a routine to practice the *drag* or *three-stroke ruff*. This is a very important rudiment that can be used in many different situations. The challenge is to play the two grace notes evenly with one hand just before playing the main note with the opposite hand. The workout starts with a simple idea and gets progressively more complicated. If you haven't practiced this rudiment in a while, spend some time warming up on it before attempting these exercises. Play each line at least four times before moving to the next.

Set Warm-Ups #1-#6
Set Fitness #14

Today's set workout will be a continuation of Set Fitness #13 on page 26. These are some more variations of sixteenth-note triplets around the set. Again, we'll use a single-stroke roll. Many of these exercises are based on a "melody line" of right-hand eighth-note triplets that is filled in with the left hand. Check out the "theme" (the first bar) and the first variation (the second bar). Notice that the right hand outlines the pattern while the left "fills it in." In #3, the three "melody notes" (1st tom, 2nd tom and floor tom) moved to different parts of the beat and the snare fills in.

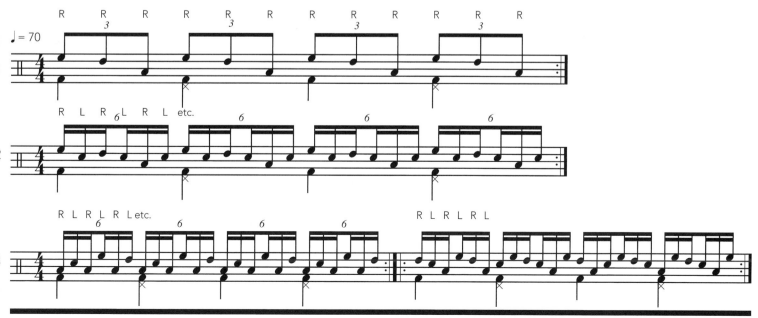

DAY FIFTEEN

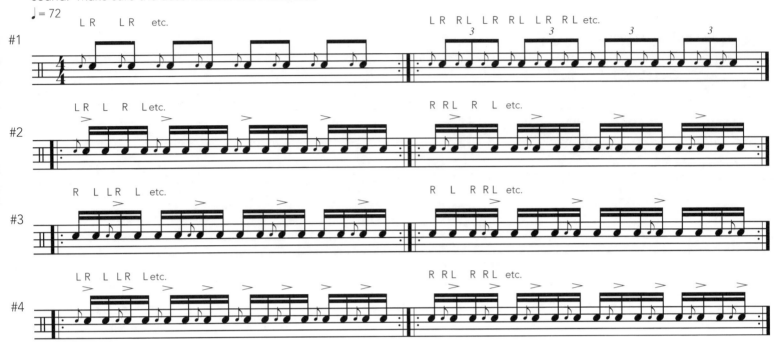

Hand Warm-Ups #1-#6
Hand Fitness #15

This workout will help you develop better control of your flams. When playing the grace note, be sure you are as close to the head as possible. Use your ear to determine if you are getting a good flam sound. Make sure the accented strokes stand out.

Set Warm-Ups #1-#6
Set Fitness #15

This workout will give you better control between the hands and bass drum. Your goal is to get a smooth flow happening between the limbs. Play quarter notes with your hi-hat throughout. Make sure the doubles in the bass drum sound even.

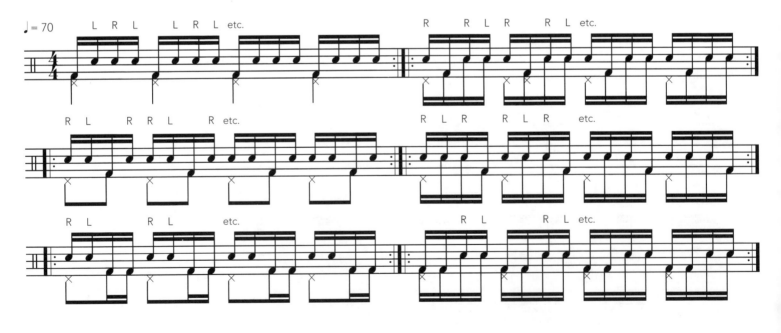

DAY SIXTEEN

Hand Warm-Ups #1-#6
Hand Fitness #16

Today's workout will help you develop the *buzz* or *press roll*. This roll is quite different from the double-stroke roll in that pressure is added to the grip to make the stick "buzz." If there is too much pressure, however, the stick won't rebound enough times to create a good "roll" sound. The first exercise below is going to help you get as many rebounds as possible in each hand. Start the stroke with a wrist motion and let the stick rebound against the head. Play each example at least four times.

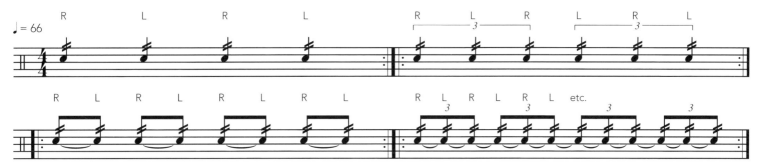

Here are a few buzz combinations to practice:

= Thirty-second notes

Set Warm-Ups #1-#6
Set Fitness #16

Today's workout is a continuation of Day Fifteen's hand and foot exercises. We'll play some of the basic figures from yesterday but today we'll double all the sixteenth notes with the bass drum, resulting in two thirty-second notes. Try playing these exercises with heel-up technique on the bass drum pedal.

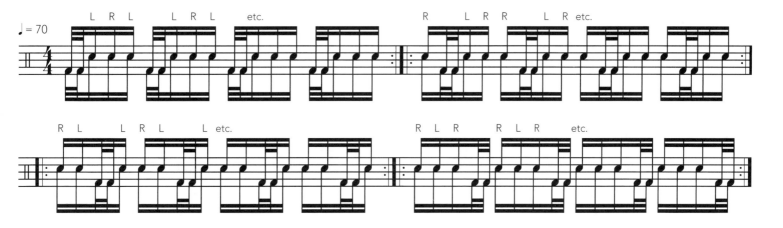

DAY SEVENTEEN

Hand Warm-Ups #1-#6
Hand Fitness #17

This workout is a continuation of Day Sixteen's buzz roll study. The idea is to play two bars of a double-stroke roll followed by two bars of a buzz roll with an eighth-note pulse. Play another two bars of doubles followed by two bars of a buzz roll with a sixteenth-note pulse. The buzz roll will begin to sound better at a faster tempo, but practice it slowly at first to help develop your ability to control the different pressures. As you gain control, increase the repetitions to four or eight bars.

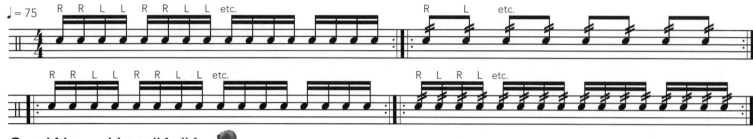

Set Warm-Ups #1-#6
Set Fitness #17

Let's take one of yesterday's exercises and *orchestrate* (designate a part of the set for each stroke) it around the full drum set. We'll take the fourth exercise from Set Fitness #16 and play it a few different ways. The stickings are only a guide to get you started and should be expanded upon after you feel comfortable.

DAY EIGHTEEN

Hand Warm-Ups #1-#6
Hand Fitness #18

Here's a workout that features two sticking ideas. The first is two bars of a single-stroke roll with a right-hand lead that changes to a left-hand lead with the insertion of a paradiddle on beat 4 of the second bar. The second sticking is two bars of double strokes that changes lead hands with the insertion of single strokes on the last two sixteenth notes of the second bar.

Set Warm-Ups #1-#6
Set Fitness #18

Below are a few more exercises that have double strokes on the bass drum. Listen for evenness.

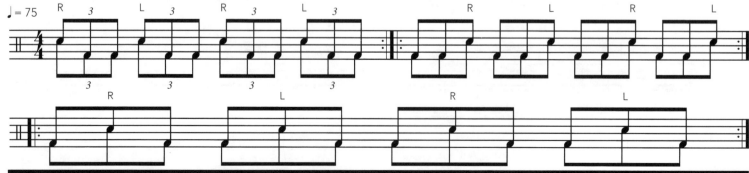

DAY NINETEEN

Hand Warm-Ups #1-#6
Hand Fitness #19

Today's workout is a continuation of Hand Fitness #18. We'll take the first sticking and work in some accent ideas. This will be challenging because the lead hand changes after two bars and so does the hand playing the accent. This opens up many possibilities for the drum set and increases your level of coordination and *ambidexterity* (playing with both hands).

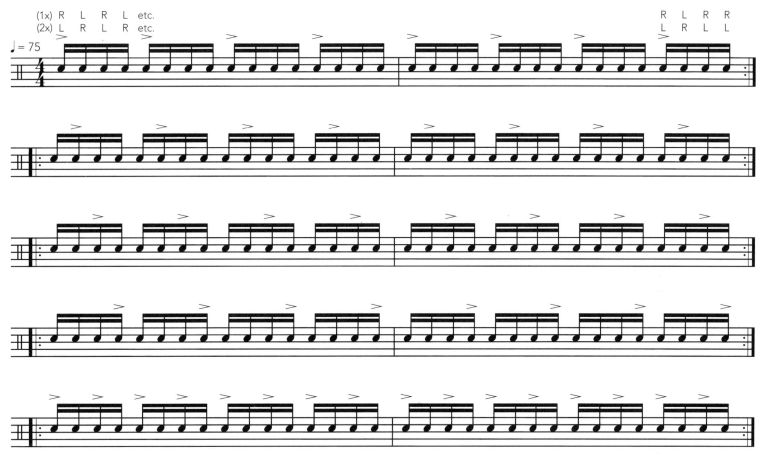

Set Warm-Ups #1-#6
Set Fitness #19

Let's take the accent and sticking patterns you worked on in today's Hand Fitness exercise and apply them to the drum set. We'll play all accented strokes on the toms and all unaccented strokes on the snare. Play right-handed accents on the floor tom; play left-hand accents on the small tom. Play quarter notes on the bass drum and add the hi-hat on beats 2 and 4. The example below shows the first accent pattern. Go ahead and play the rest of them this way, too.

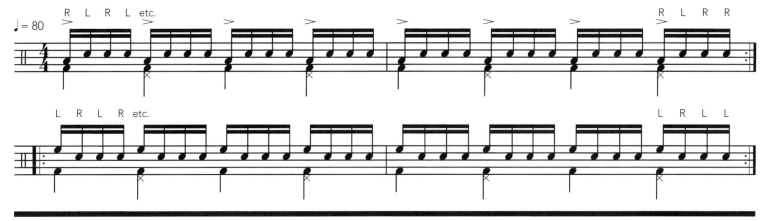

DAY TWENTY

Hand Warm-Ups #1-#6
Hand Fitness #20

This is a continuation of Hand Fitness #19. Let's take the basic idea and make it a little more interesting by playing some more challenging accent patterns. This is a very useful exercise that will help develop your ability to lead with either hand. Spend some time writing out your own accent patterns, as well. This will develop your own creativity. Also, try varying the dynamic level from very soft to very loud.

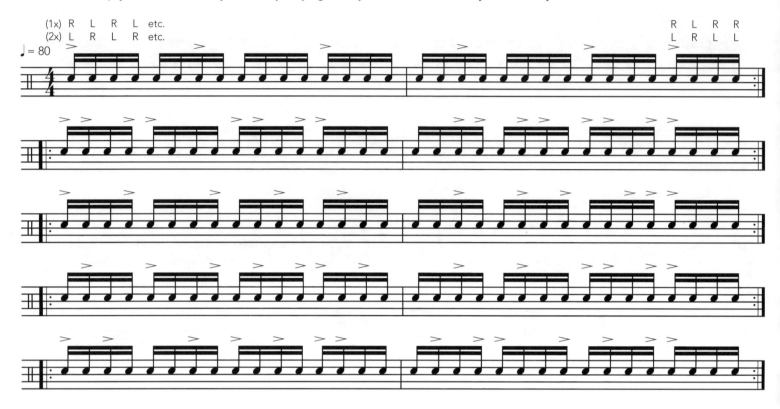

Set Warm-Ups #1-#6
Set Fitness #20

Here's another way to use the sticking and accent pattern from Set Fitness #19. Play all right-handed accents on the right crash cymbal with the bass drum, all left-handed accents with the left crash and bass drum and all unaccented strokes on the snare drum. Add the hi-hat on beats 2 and 4. The first accent pattern is shown below. Go ahead and play the rest of them (from Hand Fitness #19, page 31) this way, too.

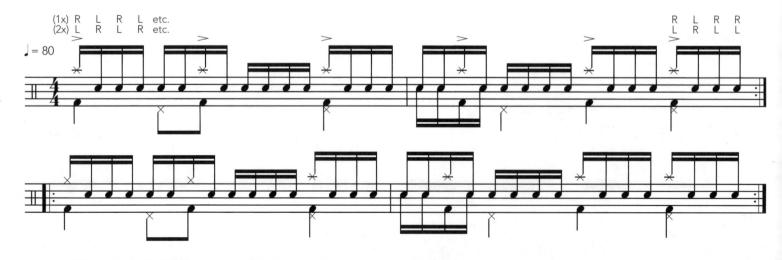

DAY TWENTY-ONE

Hand Warm-Ups #1-#6
Hand Fitness #21

Here are some accents added to the double-stroke roll sticking from Day Eighteen. Make sure the accented and unaccented strokes have lots of dynamic contrast.

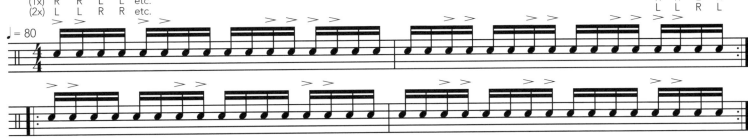

Set Warm-Ups #1-#6
Set Fitness #21

Here's an adaptation of today's Hand Fitness exercise for the drum set. This is only one possibility of many! Work up some of your own ideas using the same sticking and accent pattern.

DAY TWENTY-TWO

Hand Warm-Ups #1-#6
Hand Fitness #22

Today's workout will focus on the *four-stroke ruff*. This is a very important and much used rudiment for drummers of all styles. In a four-stroke ruff, three rapid notes, with single-stroke sticking, are inserted before the final, main, note. Here are a few stickings that will help develop your ability to lead with either hand:

Set Warm-Ups #1-#6
Set Fitness #22

Here are a few examples of the four-stroke ruff used around the drum set.

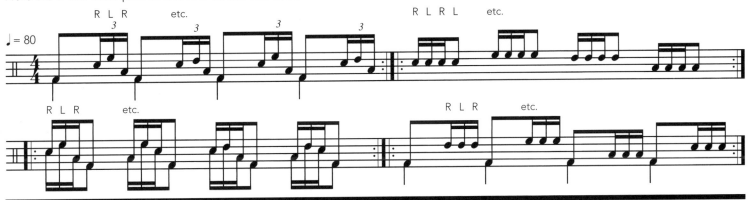

DAY TWENTY-THREE

Hand Warm-Ups #1-#6
Hand Fitness #23

Here are some triplet variations of the four-stroke ruff. They are written with a right-hand lead but should also be practiced with a left-hand lead. Play each example four times.

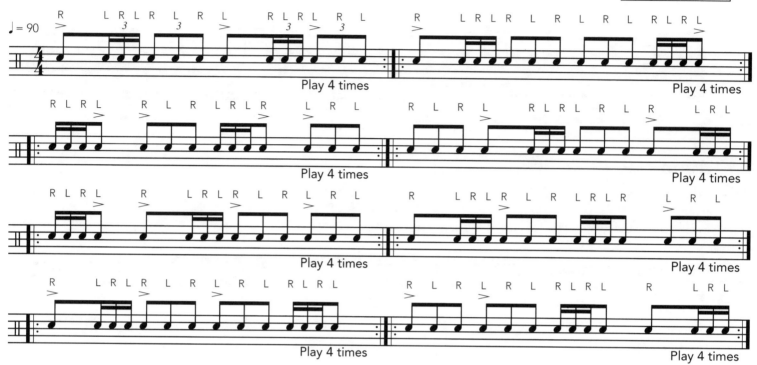

Set Warm-Ups #1-#6
Set Fitness #23

Here are some orchestrations of the four-stroke ruff including the toms. This makes for an interesting phrase that can be used in fills or solos. Once again, use a right- or left-handed lead.

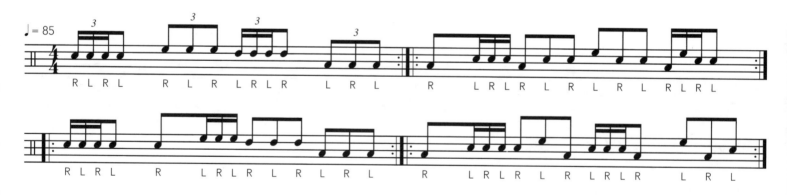

DAY TWENTY-FOUR

30 DAY DRUM WORKOUT

1	2	3	4	5	6	7
✓	✓	✓	✓	✓	✓	✓
8	9	10	11	12	13	14
✓	✓	✓	✓	✓	✓	✓
15	16	17	18	19	20	21
✓	✓	✓	✓	✓	✓	✓
22	23	24	25	26	27	28
✓	✓	✓				
29	30					

Hand Warm-Ups #1-#6
Hand Fitness #24

Today's workout will help you develop control at different dynamic levels with single-stroke-roll sticking. This exercise starts softly (***p***), *does a crescendo* (gets gradually louder) to moderately loud (***mf***) in bar 2 and then loud in bar 3 (***f***). Then it does a *decrescendo* (gets gradually softer) to the end. Try to make the changes in volume as smooth and gradual as possible. Watch your stick height for evenness. Don't get to full volume too fast!

Below is the same exercise in sixteenth-note triplets with single-stroke sticking. Try this with a left-hand lead as well.

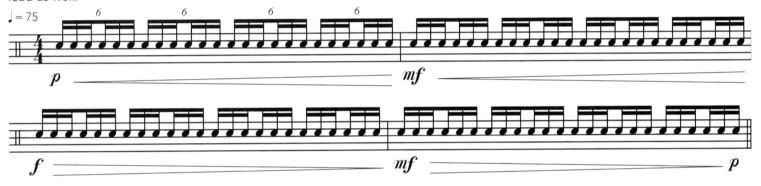

Set Warm-Ups #1-#6
Set Fitness #24

Today's workout will give you better control with a single-stroke roll between the hands and feet. There are four basic exercises in this workout that should be practiced separately and then combined to make one longer workout. This will give you the ability to lead with either hand or foot in a single-stroke roll between the snare and bass drum. This is a difficult exercise and should be worked on for a few days to build your stamina and dexterity. Play each exercise eight times. When you feel like you can do more, by all means add more bars to your workout. Don't continue if your leg cramps or becomes over-fatigued.

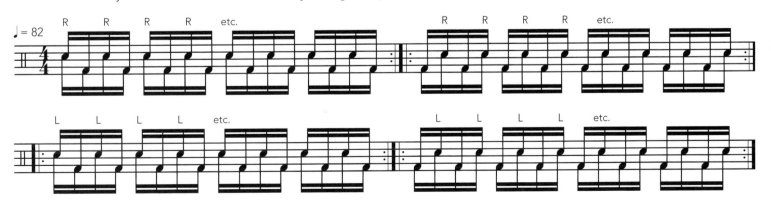

Hand Warm-Ups #1-#6
Hand Fitness #25

Here's another exercise for dynamic control. This is a single-stroke roll that begins loudly, makes a decrescendo two bars to soft and then a crescendo back to loud. Don't tighten up as you play louder.

Set Warm-Ups #1-#6
Set Fitness #25

Let's take the single-stroke snare-and-bass-drum roll from Set Fitness #24 and move the hand around the set. Start with the right hand by itself and then go to the left hand by itself. Here are two variations, but go ahead and improvise your own according to your own set up.

TWENTY-SIX

Hand Warm-Ups #1-#6
Hand Fitness #26

Today's workout will focus on *quintuplets* (five notes played in the time of four). They should be played with single-stroke-roll sticking. Listen for accuracy. Observe all accents. Play each line four times.

Play 4 times

Play 4 times

Set Warm-Ups #1-#6
Set Fitness #26

Let's add to the Set Fitness we've been working on for the past few days with a flam to the single-stroke roll. Play each bar a minimum of eight times.

DAY TWENTY-SEVEN

Hand Warm-Ups #1–#6
Hand Fitness #27

Let's add some accents to the quintuplets from Hand Fitness #26. These will be challenging, so take your time and work on playing accurately at slow tempos. This is an often-overlooked subdivision of time that is very useful. If you have difficulty with the accents, try counting the fives as follows: **1**-2-3-4-5, **2**-2-3-4-5, **3**-2-3-4-5, **4**-2-3-4-5. Eventually you will hear the rhythm and not have to count as much. Use single-stroke-roll sticking throughout. Play each example four times.

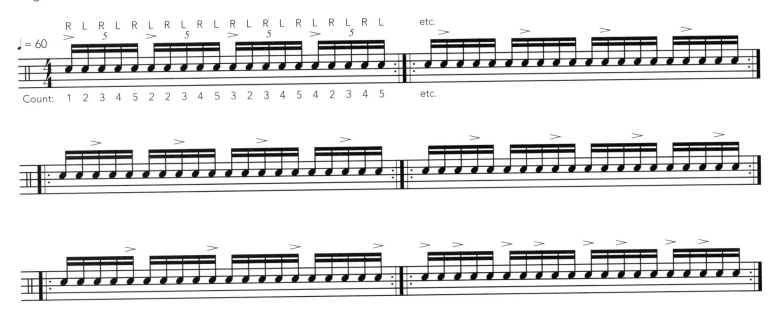

Set Warm-Ups #1–#6
Set Fitness #27

Today's workout will help you play a single-stroke roll between the hands and feet with different subdivisions of time. It starts with eighth notes, then moves to triplets, sixteenth notes and quintuplets. Play each bar eight times and then move on to the next. Play quarter notes on the hi-hat throughout. Use an alternating right-left sticking with the hands.

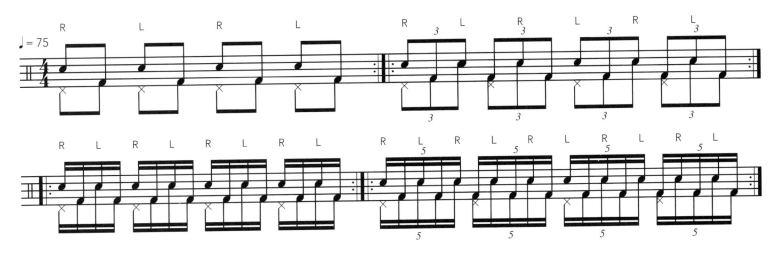

Hand Warm-Ups #1-#6
Hand Fitness #28

Today's workout is a combination of singles and doubles in three different subdivisions. This is a great workout for the hands. It begins with sixteenth notes, then moves to quintuplets and ends with sixteenth-note triplets. Play each subdivision with a single-stroke roll four times and then with a double-stroke roll four times before moving to the next line. Try playing at different dynamic levels as you perform these exercises.

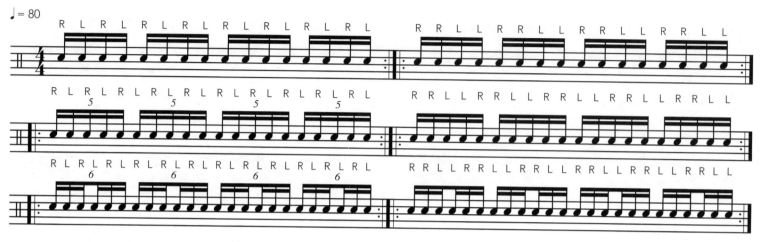

Set Warm-Ups #1-#6
Set Fitness #28

This is an application of Hand Fitness #28. Play four bars of singles and four bars of doubles between the hands and feet with different subdivisions. Start with eighth-note triplets, then move to sixteenth notes, quintuplets and sixteenth-note triplets. Use right/left sticking with the hands. You may want to vary the hi-hat part. Start by playing quarter notes and then play these exercises with no hi-hat.

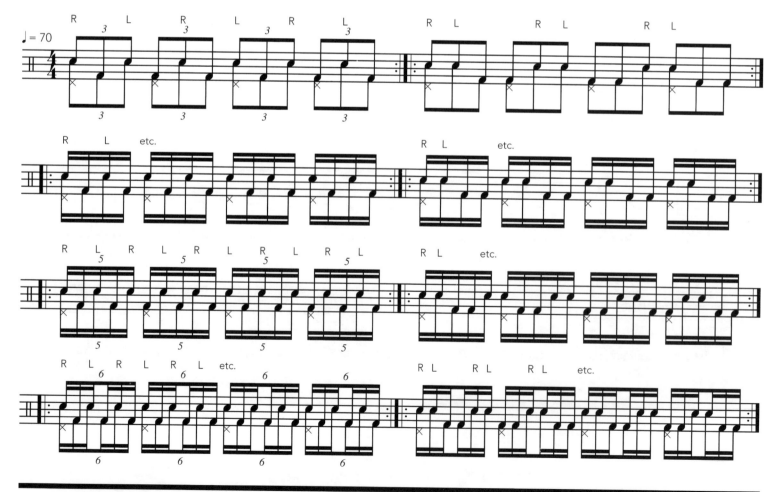

DAY TWENTY-NINE

Hand Warm-Ups #1-#6
Hand Fitness #29

Let's extend Hand Fitness #28 by adding accents to the stickings. Play the exercises accenting all right-handed strokes. Then go back and accent all left-handed strokes. Do this with every line of Hand Fitness #28. The first two lines are shown here.

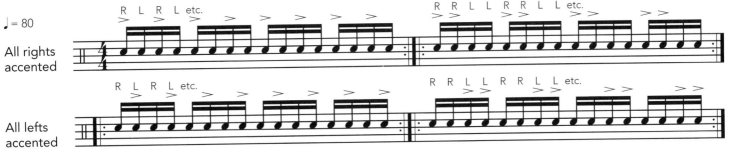

Set Warm-Ups #1-#6
Set Fitness #29

Today's workout applies Hand Fitness #29 to two drums. Play the stickings from Hand Fitness #28 and split them up between two different drums. The rights will be on the floor tom, the lefts on the snare. Play all rights as accents. Play quarter notes with the bass drum and add the hi-hat on beats 2 and 4. Then, play the rights on the snare and the lefts on the small tom with all left strokes accented. Doing this will result in some interesting *polyrhythms* (two or more rhythms played simultaneously), especially during the quintuplets. The examples with quintuplets have been written out here.

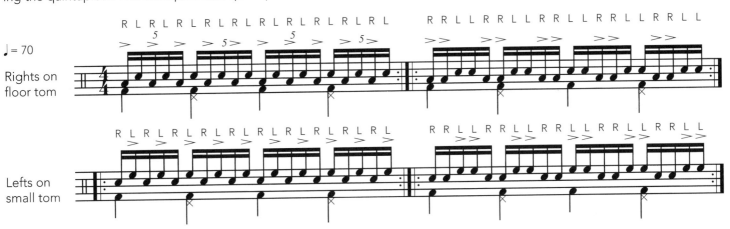

DAY THIRTY

Hand Warm-Ups #1-#6
Hand Fitness #30

Set Warm-Ups #1-#6
Set Fitness #30

Today is a review day for you. Go back and work on some of the more difficult material we have covered in the workouts. Take your time and perfect those things that are your problem areas. Remember, don't always practice the things you can already do well! Be patient. The results will come in time.

End of the Proficiency Workout

Section Five
The Extended Proficiency Workout

30 DAY DRUM WORKOUT						
1 ✓	2	3	4	5	6	7
8	9	10	11	12	13	14
15	16	17	18	19	20	21
22	23	24	25	26	27	28
29	30					

DAY ONE

Hand Warm-Ups #1-#6
Hand Fitness #1A

Let's begin the Extended Proficiency Workout with some exercises designed to increase your hand speed and stamina. The idea here is to increase the length of each exercise by one beat. We'll start with a bar of $\frac{2}{4}$, then a bar of $\frac{3}{4}$, a bar of $\frac{4}{4}$ and so on. Play each two-bar exercise eight times before moving to the next. This is a great workout for both hands! As in the Proficiency Workout, the indicated tempos are starting tempos. Begin at the tempo shown and then increase your speed from there.

Set Warm-Ups #1-#6
Set Fitness #1A

This is a workout for the bass drum combined with the hands. It involves hitting the bass and snare (with either hand) simultaneously. This is a great workout when you really crank up the tempo! When you are comfortable with the first bar, begin to play single-stroke sixteenths with both a right- and left-hand lead. Try mixing up the hi-hat part; sometimes play quarter notes, then try playing on just beats 2 and 4.

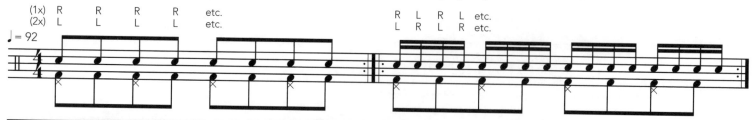

DAY TWO

Hand Warm-Ups #1-#6
Hand Fitness #2A

30 DAY DRUM WORKOUT						
1	2	3	4	5	6	7
8	9	10	11	12	13	14
15	16	17	18	19	20	21
22	23	24	25	26	27	28
29	30					

Today's workout is a series of exercises for accenting with one hand. The hands will be worked separately and then brought together. Play each bar four times before moving on to the next. Make sure there is plenty of contrast between your accented and non-accented notes. All accented notes should be at the same dynamic level, and the same is true for all unaccented strokes. Be conscious of your stick height.

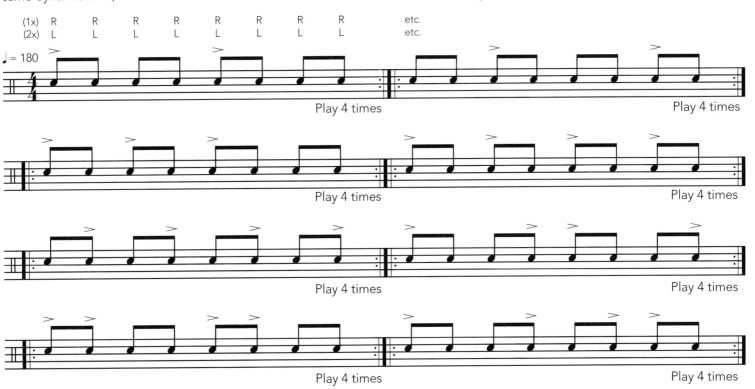

Set Warm-Ups #1-#6
Set Fitness #2A

This workout involves playing three rapid sixteenths on the bass drum. This can be quite challenging, especially at faster tempos. It may feel awkward at first, so take your time. Play the three sixteenths as evenly as possible and soon you'll have an unbelievable foot!

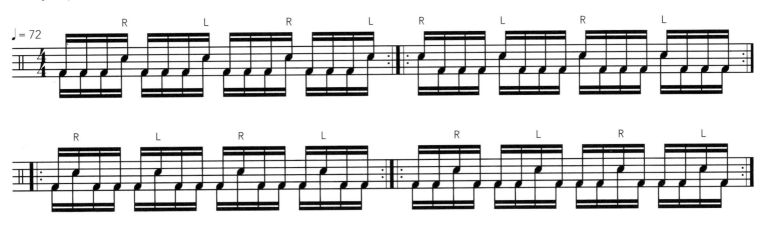

30 DAY DRUM WORKOUT						
1✓	2✓	3✓	4	5	6	7
8	9	10	11	12	13	14
15	16	17	18	19	20	21
22	23	24	25	26	27	28
29	30					

DAY THREE

Hand Warm-Ups #1-#6
Hand Fitness #3A

The following exercise uses the accent combinations from Hand Fitness #2A. Play the whole exercise with one hand, then play it with the other hand. Do this for a few days and your weaker hand is going to feel great!

Set Warm-Ups #1-#6
Set Fitness #3A

Today's workout is a combination exercise for the bass drum. We'll mix it up by playing one, two and three sixteenths on the bass drum, filling in with the snare.

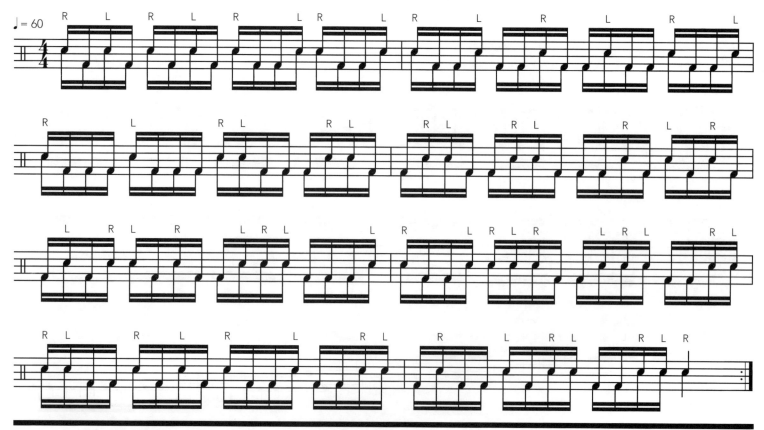

30 DAY DRUM WORKOUT						
1✓	2✓	3✓	4	5	6	7
8	9	10	11	12	13	14
15	16	17	18	19	20	21
22	23	24	25	26	27	28
29	30					

DAY FOUR

Hand Warm-Ups #1-#6
Hand Fitness #4A

This is a workout for accenting sixteenth-note triplets with a single-stroke roll. After completing this exercise with a right-hand lead, go back and do it again with a left-handed lead. Also, try playing this on the snare drum while playing quarter notes on the bass drum and adding the hi-hat on beats 2 and 4.

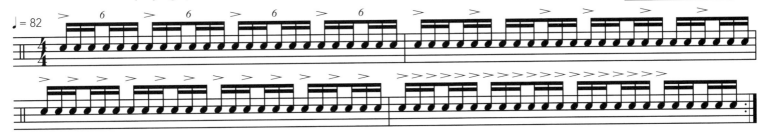

Set Warm-Ups #1-#6
Set Fitness #4A

This is a great exercise for increasing your hand to foot speed. Begin with a single-stroke roll between the snare and bass drum in sixteenth notes, then play the same figure as sixteenth-note triplets. Play another measure of sixteenths and then two measures of sixteenth-note triplets. Keep adding more bars of sixteenth-note triplets as you build endurance.

DAY FIVE

30 DAY DRUM WORKOUT						
1✓	2✓	3✓	4✓	5✓	6	7
8	9	10	11	12	13	14
15	16	17	18	19	20	21
22	23	24	25	26	27	28
29	30					

Hand Warm-Ups #1-#6
Hand Fitness #5A

This workout has a few more sixteenth-note triplet accents in addition to those from Hand Fitness #4A. Play this with both a right- and left-hand lead.

Set Warm-Ups #1-#6
Set Fitness #5A

This is a workout for playing fast double strokes with the bass drum. Try using the "heel up" method with the pedal.

DAY SIX

30 DAY DRUM WORKOUT						
1	2	3	4	5	6	7
8	9	10	11	12	13	14
15	16	17	18	19	20	21
22	23	24	25	26	27	28
29	30					

Hand Warm-Ups #1-#6
Hand Fitness #6A

Today's workout will help you play the double-stroke roll in thirty-second notes. We will progressively add more thirty-second note double-strokes to the exercise until we're playing them for one whole measure. Make sure your doubles are even and solid. Don't rely on dribbling the second stroke! Start with a wrist stroke and work it up to speed before you "go to a bounce."

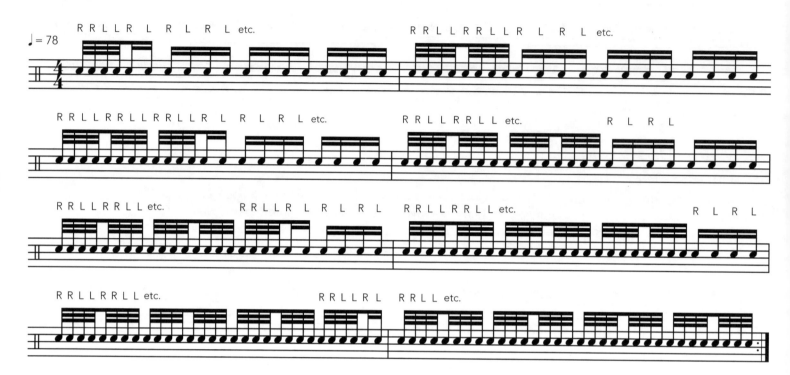

Set Warm-Ups #1-#6
Set Fitness #6A

Today's workout is a series of coordination exercises for all four limbs. They involve playing the hi-hat, bass drum, snare and ride cymbal with no two limbs playing at the same time. This is a great mental, as well as physical, challenge. All ride cymbal notes are played with the right hand and all snare drum notes are played with the left hand. Play these ideas with a nice even flow between the limbs. Be patient; this isn't going to be easy at first!

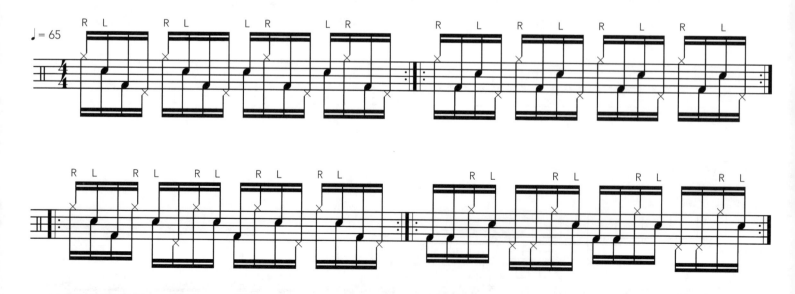

DAY SEVEN

30 DAY DRUM WORKOUT

1	2	3	4	5	6	7
✓	✓	✓	✓	✓	✓	✓
8	9	10	11	12	13	14
15	16	17	18	19	20	21
22	23	24	25	26	27	28
29	30					

Hand Warm-Ups #1-#6
Hand Fitness #7A

Today's workout will help you develop endurance with both hands. We'll start off by playing *flat flams* (simultaneous strokes on the same drum) for several minutes at a medium-slow tempo (♩ = 88). Make sure your hands hit at exactly the same time, unlike rudimental flams. This workout will be notated on a single line instead of the traditional five-line staff in order to show the relationship of the hands to each other. The right hand is the top note, the left hand is the bottom note.

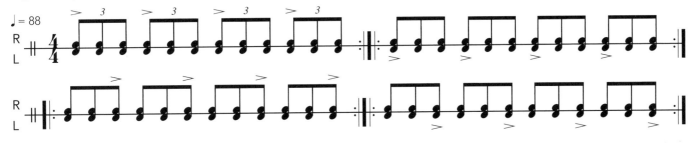

Once this feels comfortable, try playing some accents with the hands. Accents above the music are for the right hand, and accents below the music are for the left hand. If the tempo is too fast for your weaker hand, slow it down for better control. The key to developing endurance and stamina is practicing for long periods of time with relaxed muscles.

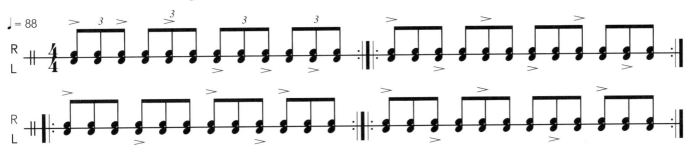

Now shift some accents from the right-hand to the left. This sounds interesting on two different drums.

Set Warm-Ups #1-#6
Set Fitness #7A

This workout provides a few triplet combinations for four-way coordination. Take it slowly at first and play these evenly.

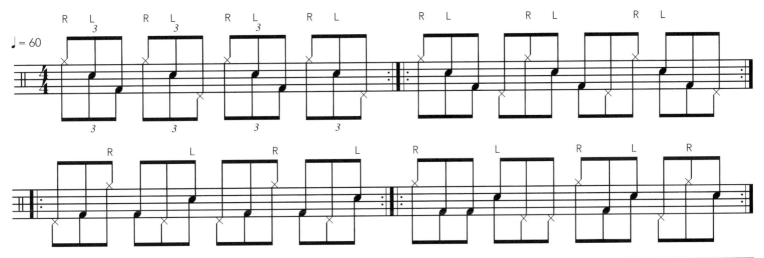

30 DAY DRUM WORKOUT

1	2	3	4	5	6	7
✓	✓	✓	✓	✓	✓	✓
8 ✓	9	10	11	12	13	14
15	16	17	18	19	20	21
22	23	24	25	26	27	28
29	30					

DAY EIGHT

Hand Warm-Ups #1–#6
Hand Fitness #8A

Let's continue today with more accents for flat flams. These workouts are great for developing evenness between the hands. They are also excellent for coordination.

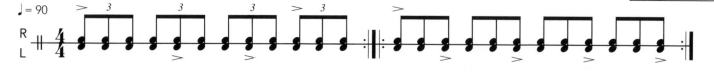

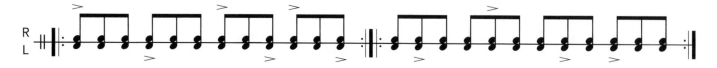

Here are a few examples with sixteenth notes:

Set Warm-Ups #1–#6
Set Fitness #8A

Today's workout will explore a few possibilities for paradiddle sticking around the set. There are some unusual variations here, so take your time and learn the orchestrations first. Then, play them faster.

30 DAY DRUM WORKOUT

1	2	3	4	5	6	7
8	9	10	11	12	13	14
15	16	17	18	19	20	21
22	23	24	25	26	27	28
29	30					

DAY NINE

Hand Warm-Ups #1-#6
Hand Fitness #9A

For the next three days we'll work on the rudimental flam with some variations. Today's workout will focus on the flam with single-stroke-roll sticking in triplets. Experiment with the placement of the grace note, from very open (loose, or far from the main note) to very close (tight, or near the main note).

Set Warm-Ups #1-#6
Set Fitness #9A

This workout has doubles (double strokes, RR LL) around the set in triplets. Play quarter notes on the bass drum adding the hi-hat on beats 2 and 4. These are very polyrhythmic. To keep from losing your place, be sure to count as you play.

30 DAY DRUM WORKOUT

1	2	3	4	5	6	7
8	9	10	11	12	13	14
15	16	17	18	19	20	21
22	23	24	25	26	27	28
29	30					

DAY TEN

Hand Warm-Ups #1-#6
Hand Fitness #10A

Today's workout continues with some flam exercises in sixteenth notes. Observe all the sticking indications.

Set Warm-Ups #1-#6
Set Fitness #10A

Here are more double-strokes broken up around the set:

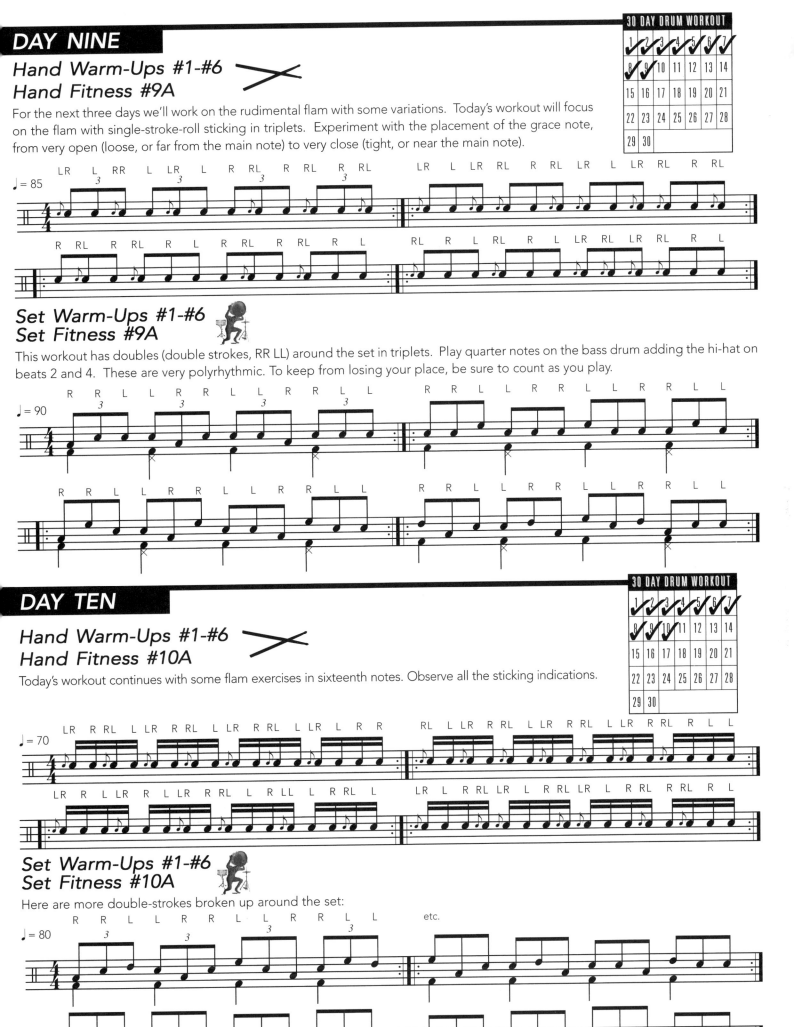

SECTION FIVE—The Extended Proficiency Workout   47

30 DAY DRUM WORKOUT

1	2	3	4	5	6	7
✓	✓	✓	✓	✓	✓	✓
8	9	10	11	12	13	14
✓	✓	✓	✓			
15	16	17	18	19	20	21
22	23	24	25	26	27	28
29	30					

Hand Warm-Ups #1-#6
Hand Fitness #11A

Today's workout was created by the great drummer, Dave Calarco. This one is difficult because the accent occurs on every fourth stroke, just as you change lead hands. This is quite challenging at a fast tempo!

Set Warm-Ups #1-#6
Set Fitness #11A

This workout is an application of flams to the drum set. We'll take some flam ideas and play them between the snare drum and crash cymbals, with the bass drum reinforcing the accented notes. This is a tremendous workout for the arms! After mastering this, you'll have no problem reaching up to the crash cymbals!

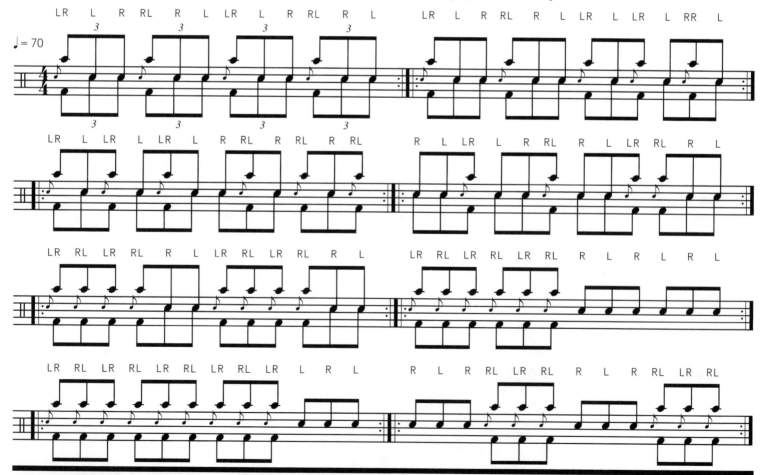

DAY TWELVE

Hand Warm-Ups #1-#6
Hand Fitness #12A

Today's workout will focus on dynamics. These exercises will increase your control and sensitivity at different dynamic levels. Play through each exercise until you perfect the indicated dynamics. After you have done this, go back and work on each exercise with as many different dynamic levels as you can think of. Dynamic contrast will make your playing sound more musical and interesting.

pp = Pianissimo (Very Soft)
ff = Fortissimo (Very Loud)

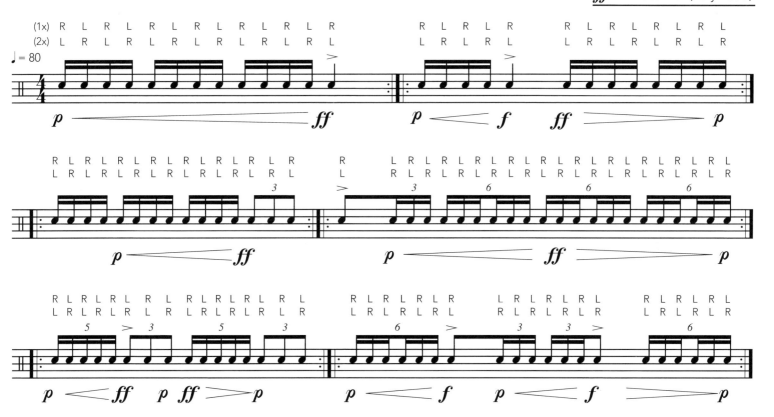

Set Warm-Ups #1-#6
Set Fitness #12A

This is a workout for crossing the hands around the set. We'll use single-stroke-roll sticking throughout, and the hand that crosses will be indicated with a circle around the sticking. This is a great workout for getting around the drums!

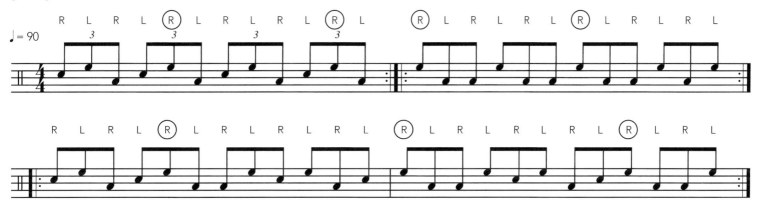

Hand Warm-Ups #1-#6
Hand Fitness #13A

Let's continue with more exercises for dynamic control. Observe all of the sticking and dynamic markings. On the crescendo examples, be sure that each stroke is a little louder than the previous one. Make sure you don't hit your peak volume too soon! On the decrescendos, it's just the opposite—don't play too soft too soon. Make very gradual dynamic changes.

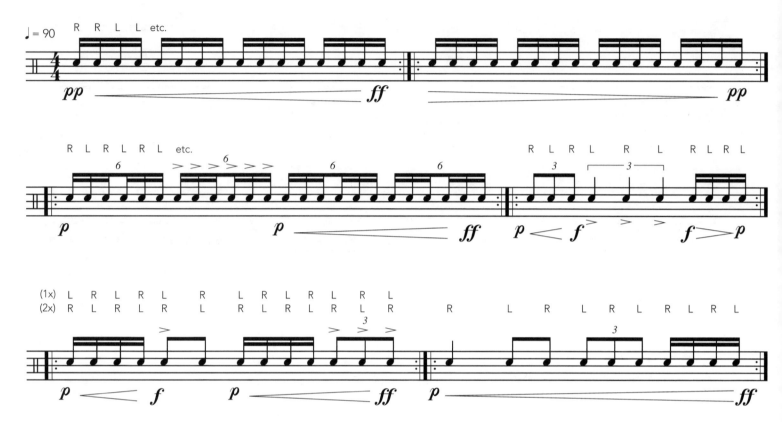

Set Warm-Ups #1-#6
Set Fitness #13A

This workout continues with more cross-handed studies. Today, we'll mix up triplets and sixteenths in a four-bar phrase. Use single-stroke-roll sticking.

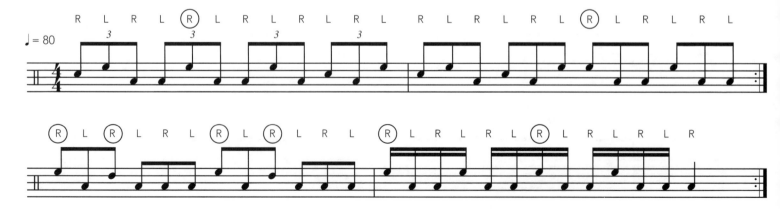

DAY FOURTEEN

Hand Warm-Ups #1-#6
Hand Fitness #14A

Today's workout comprises two triplet exercises with paradiddle sticking. These patterns create cyclical two-bar phrases. Try playing them with and without accents. The accents create a polyrhythm by forming a half-note triplet within the sticking. In other words, the accents evenly divide the measure into three groups of four triplet eighth notes. Phrase marks are included to clarify the polyrhythms.

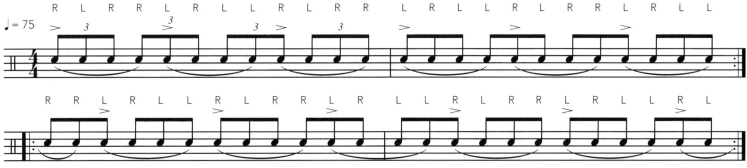

Set Warm-Ups #1-#6
Set Fitness #14A

Let's adapt Hand Fitness #14A to the drum set. The first sticking from the exercise above is written out with the bass drum playing quarter notes and the hi-hat added on beats 2 and 4. The half-note-triplet phrasing is orchestrated around the toms. The second adaptation has the half-note-triplet phrasing on the bass drum and crash cymbals. Count!

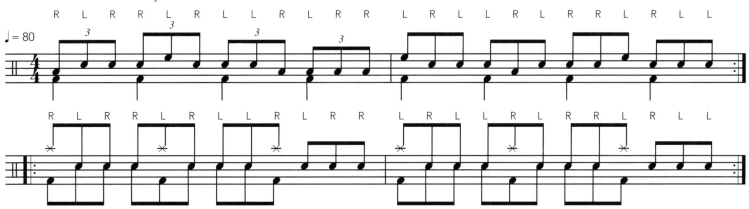

DAY FIFTEEN

Hand Warm-Ups #1-#6
Set Warm-Ups #1-#6
Hand Fitness and Set Fitness #15A

Today is a review day for you. It's time to go back and review any of the material that was either difficult for you or that needs better control or speed. You may also want to compose your own variations on various exercises that appeal to you. Find ways that this material can be adapted to your particular playing situations. This is the real value of studying technical material: finding ways to use it in a musical rather than purely "drumistic" way. Many drummers get so wrapped up in how fast they can play that they lose sight of the melodic and groove aspects of playing the drums. The technical studies are there to help you gain control and inspire new ideas, thus increasing your performance options.

Also, be aware of how you go about practicing and developing new material. You must be critical of your progress and manage your time well. Many books and videos show you *what* to practice, but not *how* to practice. This is a very individual thing and no two people go about it the same way. The keys are self-discipline, patience and desire. You must have long-term and short-term goals that you're constantly working towards. All progress on any instrument is generally made in small steps over long periods of time. That is why it is so important to have an organized approach, where wasted time and effort are held to a minimum. Practice must be enjoyable or you will not spend the necessary time doing it! Find ways to make it fun and productive.

DAY SIXTEEN

Hand Warm-Ups #1-#6
Hand Fitness #16A

Let's call today's workout "The Accelerator." This is a single-stroke-roll exercise that gives the illusion of speeding up by playing progressively smaller note values. In the first exercise, we'll work on playing each note value for two beats. When you feel comfortable with that, move to the second exercise which has the note values changing on every beat. The third exercise is "The De-accelerator," which starts with the smaller values and moves to larger values. These exercises are great for your single-stroke chops!

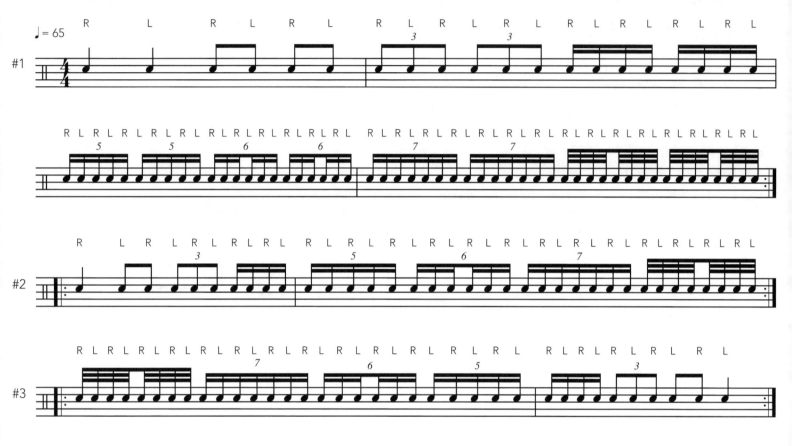

Set Warm-Ups #1-#6
Set Fitness #16A

Here's a workout for *double stops* on the drum set. Double stops are basically flat flams played between two drums. These exercises are tremendous for your arms and wrists. Start at the indicated tempo and work it up to a Tony Williams tempo!

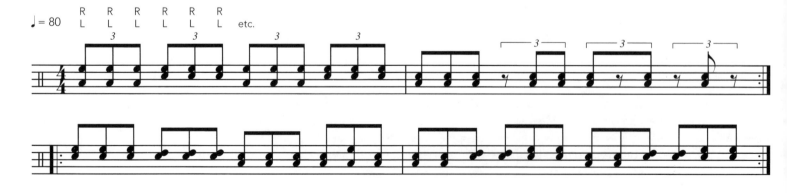

DAY SEVENTEEN

Hand Warm-Ups #1-#6
Set Warm-Ups #1-#6
Hand Fitness and Set Fitness #17A

30 DAY DRUM WORKOUT						
1✓	2✓	3✓	4✓	5✓	6✓	7✓
8✓	9✓	10✓	11✓	12✓	13✓	14✓
15✓	16✓	17✓	18	19	20	21
22	23	24	25	26	27	28
29	30					

Today will be a combination day for both the hands and feet. This workout will focus on playing double-stroke-roll combinations over an *ostinato* (a repeated accompaniment pattern) with bass drum and hi-hat. Start by playing this rhythm with the feet:

Now play the following roll patterns on the snare drum. Observe all sticking indications.

Now go back and play the workout with a left-hand lead. Try varying your dynamics.

Hand Warm-Ups #1-#6
Hand Fitness #18A

Today's hand fitness is called "The Push." It is designed to help your single strokes by adding one beat of quicker notes at the end of the measure. This way you have to "push" the single stroke faster but only for one beat. After you play it with a right-hand lead, immediately change over to a left-hand lead.

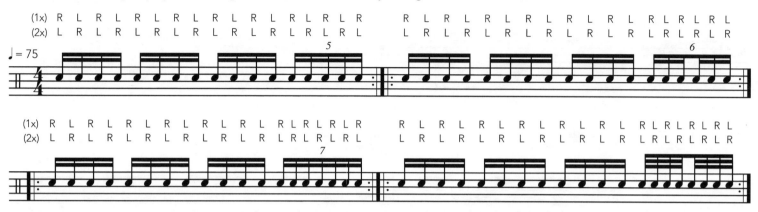

As you become more proficient with this workout, start to add more beats of quicker notes. Here is an example using quintuplets:

Set Warm-Ups #1-#6
Set Fitness #18A

This is a workout for four-way single strokes. The idea is to play singles starting with either hand or foot. If you wish, you can substitute the hi-hat for the bass drum.

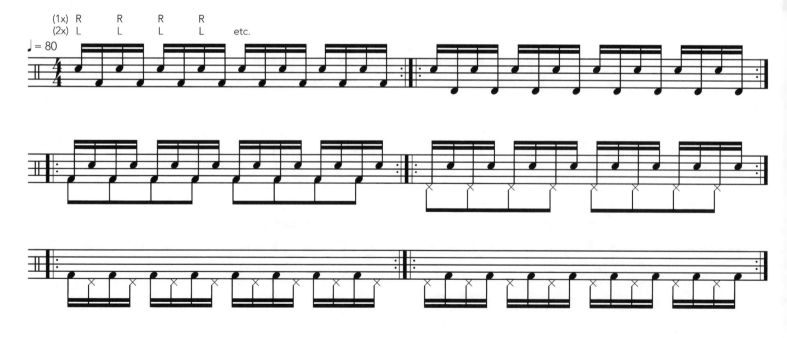

DAY NINETEEN

30 DAY DRUM WORKOUT

1	2	3	4	5	6	7
8	9	10	11	12	13	14
15	16	17	18	19	20	21
22	23	24	25	26	27	28
29	30					

Hand Warm-Ups #1-#6
Set Warm-Ups #1-#6
Hand Fitness and Set Fitness #19A

For the next two days, we'll combine hand fitness and set fitness and focus on *bass drum substitutions*. This is a process in which we use the bass drum to replace a note that was played by a hand. All of the following examples will be based on a single-stroke roll. Let's start with a sixteenth-note single-stroke roll and then replace a few of the strokes with the bass drum, but leave the sticking intact.

Here is a workout featuring this idea:

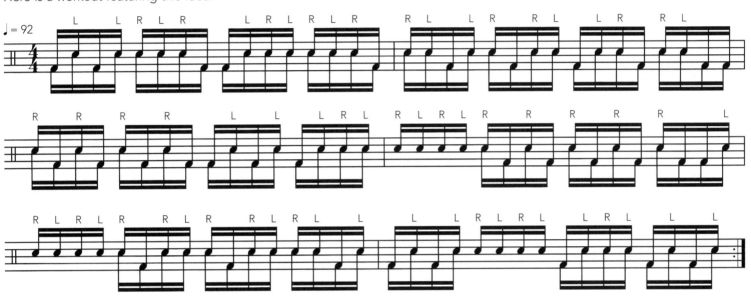

DAY TWENTY

30 DAY DRUM WORKOUT

1	2	3	4	5	6	7
8	9	10	11	12	13	14
15	16	17	18	19	20	21
22	23	24	25	26	27	28
29	30					

Hand Warm-Ups #1-#6
Set Warm-Ups #1-#6
Hand Fitness and Set Fitness #20A

This is a workout for bass-drum substitutions in triplets. After you gain control over this material, expand the workout by playing the hi-hat on different beats and orchestrating the phrases around the drum set. Try substituting the hi-hat for the bass drum. Use your own creativity to make these exercises musical and interesting.

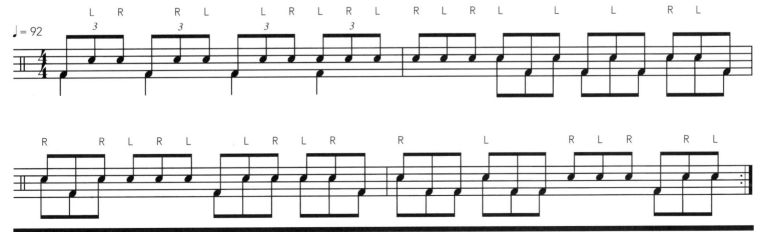

Hand Warm-Ups #1-#6
Set Warm-Ups #1-#6
Hand Fitness and Set Fitness #21A

Today we will begin a series of workout days that will feature ostinatos for either the hands or feet. The idea is to perform a repetitive rhythm with one or two limbs while playing a series of exercises with the other limbs. This will increase your sense of coordination, balance and time. Today's workout will be an ostinato study in $\frac{3}{4}$ time. Begin by playing this ostinato with the bass drum and stepped hi-hat.

♩ = 120

When you feel comfortable with the ostinato rhythm, play this workout with the hands while playing the ostinato with the feet. It is a good idea to play this hand exercise without the ostinato as well.

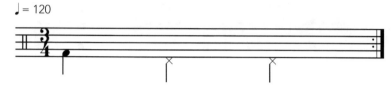

Try taking this workout further by substituting one of these ostinatos for the one above.

DAY TWENTY-TWO

30 DAY DRUM WORKOUT						
1✓	2✓	3✓	4✓	5✓	6✓	7✓
8✓	9✓	10✓	11✓	12✓	13✓	14
15✓	16✓	17✓	18✓	19✓	20✓	21✓
22✓	23	24	25	26	27	28
29	30					

Hand Warm-Ups #1-#6
Set Warm-Ups #1-#6
Hand Fitness and Set Fitness #22A

These exercises are presented as an *etude* (a piece devoted to a particular technique). If you have difficulty playing through the whole etude, study each bar separately first before playing the whole. The first ostinato is a *Baion,* a popular dance rhythm from northern Brazil. It is played between the bass drum and stepped hi-hat.

In the etude below, play the Baion ostinato as you play the hands on the snare drum.

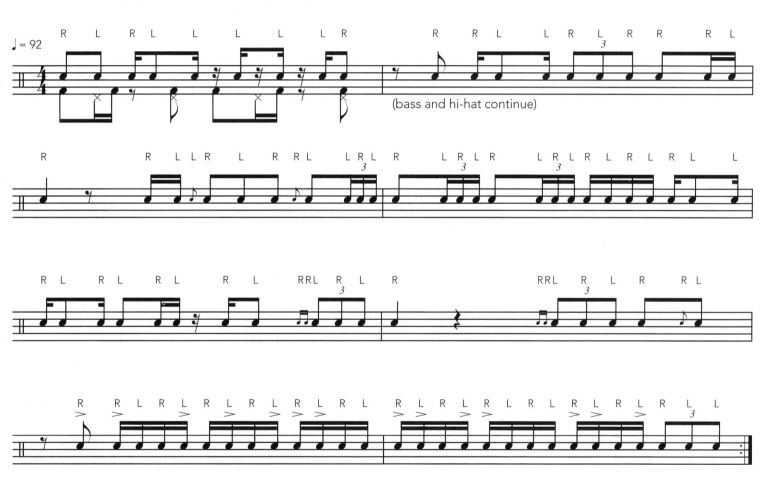

(bass and hi-hat continue)

DAY TWENTY-THREE

30 DAY DRUM WORKOUT

1	2	3	4	5	6	7
8	9	10	11	12	13	14
15	16	17	18	19	20	21
22	23	24	25	26	27	28
29	30					

Hand Warm-Ups #1-#6
Set Warm-Ups #1-#6
Hand Fitness and Set Fitness #23A

Today's workout will feature rudimental roll exercises for the snare and bass drums. First, work through the basic variations. This will help you develop even rolls and improve your ability to accent with the bass drum.

7 = The number above the roll indicates the amount of strokes. For example, this is a seven-stroke roll.

Now try these variations with roll patterns. Begin at the indicated tempo and work up from there.

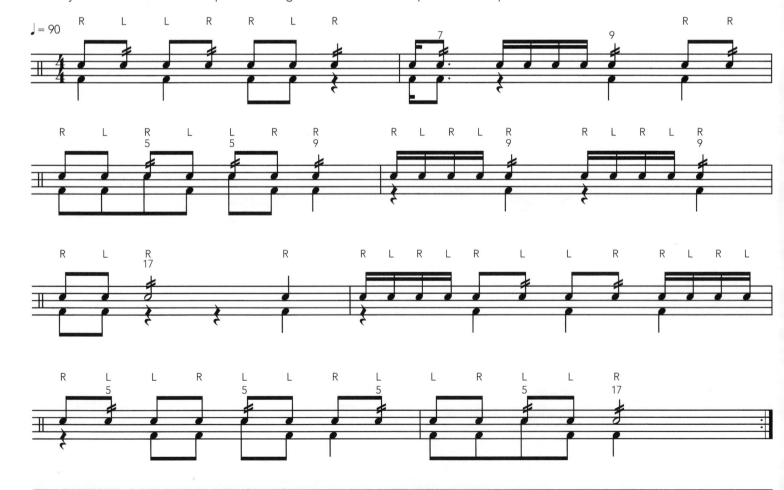

30 DAY DRUM WORKOUT

1	2	3	4	5	6	7
8	9	10	11	12	13	14
15	16	17	18	19	20	21
22	23	24	25	26	27	28
29	30					

DAY TWENTY-FOUR

Hand Warm-Ups #1-#6
Set Warm-Ups #1-#6
Hand Fitness and Set Fitness #24A

This is a very challenging workout. Set your metronome to ♩ = 50. Play quarter notes with single-stroke sticking. Make sure you lock in tightly with the click. Then, play eighth notes for four bars, triplets for four bars and sixteenth notes for four bars. This is a great workout for developing a feel for playing the spaces between the notes evenly at a slow tempo. It's also great for making the transitions from one note value to another at a slow tempo. This workout is all about being able to play slowly. When you feel comfortable at ♩ = 50, try ♩ = 42. Eventually, try ♩ = 35. If you want to have some real fun, try playing quarter-note triplets at this tempo! This workout will greatly improve your rhythm.

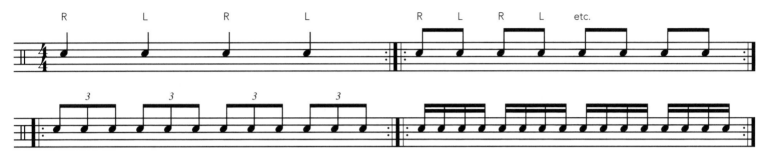

DAY TWENTY-FIVE

30 DAY DRUM WORKOUT

1	2	3	4	5	6	7
8	9	10	11	12	13	14
15	16	17	18	19	20	21
22	23	24	25	26	27	28
29	30					

Hand Warm-Ups #1-#6
Set Warm-Ups #1-#6
Hand Fitness and Set Fitness #25A

Today is another review day for you. It's time to go back and practice material you found to be difficult. Take this time to advance the tempos of the exercises you have been practicing.

This is also a good time to develop your powers of concentration. Try some "distraction practice." When we perform in a live situation, there are generally many distractions coming from all directions. Yet when we practice, we sit in a room by ourselves—without distractions. To improve your ability to concentrate and the strength of your inner clock, create some artificial distraction. Play any of the workouts with a metronome, and turn a radio on, set to any random station. Continue to stay with the click rather than go with the tempo of whatever is being played on the radio. Here's the fun part: Turn off the metronome but continue to play that tempo and ignore what you hear on the radio. All the while, maintain the form of the exercise (length in bars, repeats, etc.) for a few minutes. Then, turn the metronome back on and check yourself. This will strengthen your sense of time and you will be less likely to lose the tempo in a live situation due to concentration problems.

DAY TWENTY-SIX

Hand Warm-Ups #1-#6
Set Warm-Ups #1-#6
Hand Fitness and Set Fitness #26A

Today's workout is a study in "tuplets" over two beats. In the case of an eighth-note quintuplet (five evenly spaced notes in the time of two beats), start by playing sixteenth-note quintuplets (five evenly spaced notes in the time of one beat, #1) and then add accents on all of the right-hand strokes (#2). Finally, omit the left-hand strokes and you will have five notes in the time of two beats (#3). On your own, try eighth-note septuplets (seven evenly spaced notes in the time of two beats); play sixteenth-note septuplets (seven notes per beat) accenting the right-hand strokes, then remove the left-hand strokes, and you have seven notes in the time of two beats. Remember, you can think of the tuplets as being polyrhythms. For example, the quarter-note quintuplet can be thought of as 5:2 (five against two).

Once you feel comfortable with this concept, master the exercise below with single-stroke sticking. Play quarter notes on the bass drum with the hi-hat added on beats 2 and 4. Practice this with a metronome! If you have a metronome that you can set to accent certain beats, accent the first beat of a ²⁄₄ bar so you have a nice reminder of where beat 1 is. It is helpful not only to count the beat (quarter-note pulse) but the subdivisions as well. Remember, these are groups of notes *evenly spaced* over two beats. Counting will help you achieve that correct spacing. Be patient! It may take some time for these exercises to feel comfortable. They are very usable but you must be able to hear them clearly in your "mind's ear" before they are of any use to you musically. Try recording yourself to hear if you are performing these correctly.

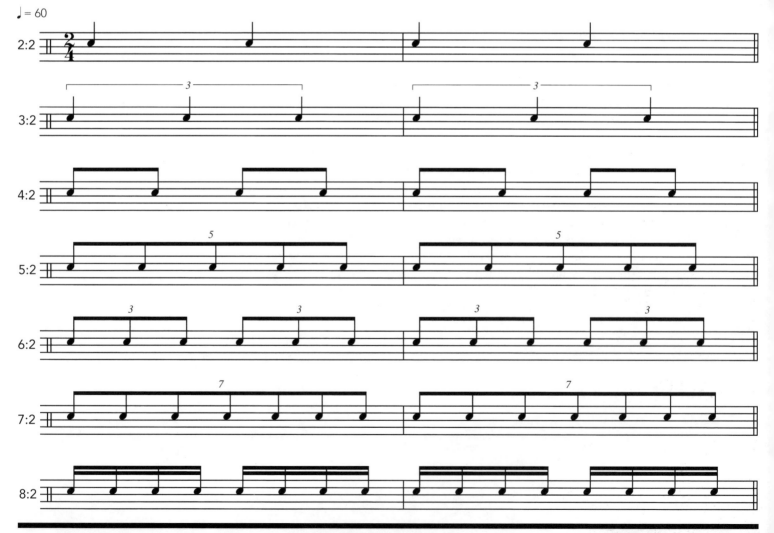

DAY TWENTY-SEVEN

Hand Warm-Ups #1-#6
Set Warm-Ups #1-#6
Hand Fitness and Set Fitness #27A

This is a workout for polyrhythms in the time of three beats. This will be a challenge, mostly due to the fact that this is uncommon. To learn to hear and play these, it is helpful to be able to set your metronome to accent beat 1 of a $\frac{3}{4}$ bar. Here's an example: Play quintuplets in $\frac{3}{4}$ with single-stroke-roll sticking. Accent the quintuplet in groups of three, starting with the first stroke. Remove all of the unaccented notes and you have the polyrhythm of five in the time of three (5 against 3—5:3). As a reference for you, this process has been outlined above each of the different polyrhythms in this workout. Master each polyrhythm before moving on to the next. Notice that for 8:3, you must play accented thirty-second notes, which are twice as fast as sixteenth notes (eight notes per beat). Phrase marks are added for clarification.

$\quad\quad \downarrow = 65$

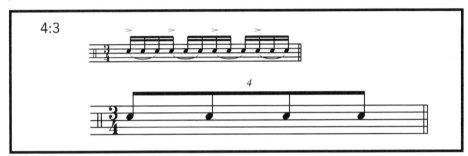

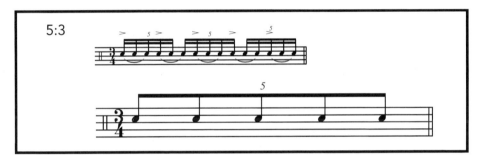

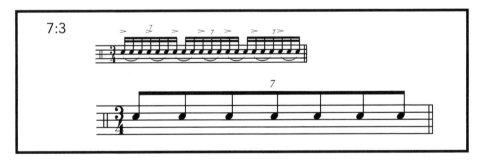

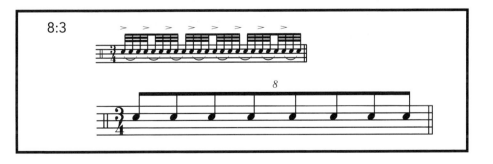

Hand Warm-Ups #1-#6
Set Warm-Ups #1-#6
Hand Fitness and Set Fitness #28A

Today's workout is a rudiments etude. This solo will cover some of the more common roll patterns, like the seven- and nine-stroke rolls. The bass drum will contribute to accenting phrases. If you're not already, try spending some time working through rudimental snare drum material when you practice. It's great for your chops and reading ability. Observe all stickings.

DAY TWENTY-NINE

Hand Warm-Ups #1-#6
Set Warm-Ups #1-#6
Hand Fitness and Set Fitness #29A

This is a workout for the hands and feet in "call and response" phrasing. The hands play an idea and the feet either mimic the idea or answer it with a similar phrase. This is a good way to build up your improvising skills. Don't stop with the exercises presented here. Rather, take the concept and create your own ideas. That is really the whole point.

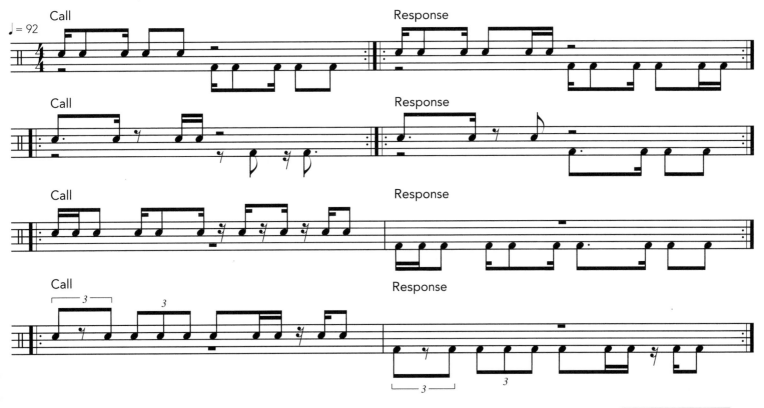

DAY THIRTY

Hand Warm-Ups #1-#6
Set Warm-Ups #1-#6
Hand Fitness and Set Fitness #30A

This is a workout for *after* a gig, rehearsal or practice session. The idea is to warm down, very much like horn players do. If you can fit this in, you're going to see some great results. The exercise should be played slowly and with full strokes for a period of five minutes after a performance. This will loosen up the muscles in the arms, wrists and hands.

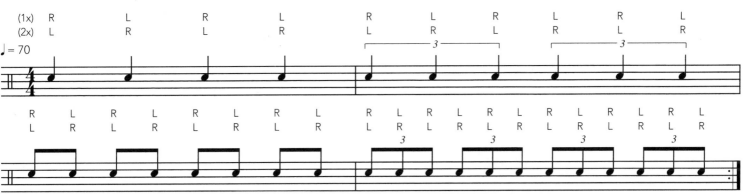

End of the Proficiency Workout